Leaving Ukraine

How Putin's invasion changed one boy's life

By Sue Johns

SUE JOHNS

First edition, 2024, *Leaving Ukraine: How Putin's invasion changed one boy's life*

Copyright © Sue Johns 2024

All rights reserved. No part of the publication may be reproduced, stored in a retrieval system, transmitted or circulated in any form or by any means, electronic, mechanical, photocopying, recording or otherwise, without prior permission in writing from the author. For permissions contact the author: sue@kingsway-house.co.uk

Although every precaution has been taken to verify the accuracy of the information contained herein, the author assumes no responsibility for any errors or omissions. No liability is assumed for losses or damages that may result from the use of information contained within. You are responsible for your own choices, actions and results.

A CIP catalogue record for this book is available from the British Library.

ISBN: 978-1-0685045-0-1 (paperback)

ISBN: 978-1-0685045-1-8 (e-book)

Cover design: Harvey Fitzhugh at Sleep.Create.Repeat.

Contents

Contents 3
Author's Notes 5
Chapter 1 Kyiv, Ukraine – February 2022 9
Chapter 2 Ombersley, UK – February 2022 15
Chapter 3 Kyiv, Ukraine – February 2022 24
Chapter 4 Ombersley, UK – February 2022 32
Chapter 5 Poland – February 2022 38
Chapter 6 Ombersley, UK – March 2022 43
Chapter 7 Poland - March 2022 50
Chapter 8 Ombersley, UK – March 2022 56
Chapter 9 Germany and Switzerland 69
Chapter 10 UK March – April 2022 75
Chapter 11 Switzerland – March 2022 85
Chapter 12 To Paris March – April 2022 93
Chapter 13 UK March – April 2022 99
Chapter 14 UK April 2022 104
Chapter 15 To Worcester April 2022 110
Chapter 16 Settling In 117
Chapter 17 Leisure Time 123
Chapter 18 Charming the Locals 129
Chapter 19 Independent Thinking 134
Chapter 20 Give and Take 143

Chapter 21 Parental Distance 149

Chapter 22 Holidays 154

Chapter 23 Summer Jobs 161

Chapter 24 Sixth Form Graduation 166

Chapter 25 Feedback from Hosts 172

Chapter 26 Kyiv, Ukraine – July 2024 185

Chapter 27 Ukraine – November 2024 191

Acknowledgements 195

Author's Notes

Yurii's Point of View

The main character in the story is Yurii (pronounced /you-ree/). Part One of Leaving Ukraine is based on his own account, which he told me in various conversations over a period of about six months. He knew that I was recording our conversations and that the information he gave me would form the basis of my book. He was happy to oblige but, of course, being Yurii, he wanted to know if he would become famous as a result! All conversations Yurii has throughout the book are based on what he told me, with some imagined elements added. After reading the book he texted me the following: 'I finished reading the book. I love it! I don't think Ombersley part is boring. I found it even more entertaining than the journey.'

Sources of Information

In addition to about six hours of recorded conversations with Yurii, I had video calls with his father, with Mathieu (the young Swiss man whom Yurii stayed with en route to the UK) and with Carla, who looked after him in Paris. They were all happy to help me piece together Yurii's journey and knew my ultimate aim was to write a book. I have also referred to emails, texts and WhatsApp messages with various people during the period when I was trying to get Yurii and others to the UK.

Spelling is Political

The process of converting one writing system to another is called 'transliteration' and this is what happens when Ukrainian names are written in English. Mapping one alphabet onto a different one often leads to variations in spelling, which explains why there might be different spellings for the same word.

In addition Russian and Ukrainian alphabets are slightly different, resulting in slightly different transliterations of proper nouns, such as:

Kyiv (Ukrainian) and Kiev (Russian)

Odesa (Ukrainian) and Odessa (Russian)

Dnipro (Ukrainian) and Dnieper (Russian)

Volodymyr (Ukrainian) and Vladimir (Russian)

Oleksandr (Ukrainian) and Aleksandr (Russian)

Before Putin's invasion of Ukraine, British English spelling tended to favour the Russian version of names and spoken English used the Russian pronunciation. After the invasion, the BBC and other broadcasters started using the Ukrainian pronunciation /Keev/ rather than the Russian version, /Ki-ev/. Due to the subject matter of this book, I have used Ukrainian spellings where appropriate.

To make it easier for native English speakers, I have used English translations of street names in Ukraine and Poland.

PART ONE

February–April 2022

YURII'S JOURNEY

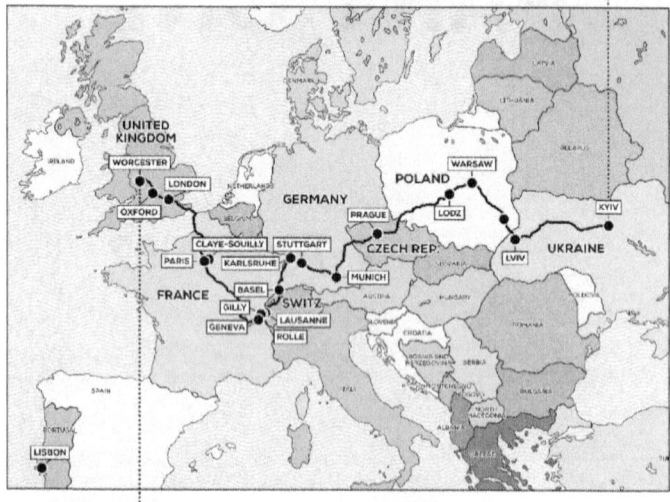

Chapter 1
Kyiv, Ukraine – February 2022

Standing by the school gates was a tall, skinny sixteen-year-old with spiky hair. He'd been amongst the first pupils to be discharged from School Number 194 'Perspective', and was now waiting for his friend who'd probably be amongst the last. At over six feet tall the boy, Yurii, could have been a model in a parallel universe, but today his demeanour lacked the swagger necessary for the catwalk. His eyes were missing their usual sparkle and his hunched posture was indicative of cold or misery. The knot in his stomach hadn't shifted for days so he'd skipped lunch and the sandwich remained un-touched in his backpack. He watched blankly as the trickle of pupils turned into a surge which gradually dissipated along Heroes of the Dnipro Street. Both the school's name and address contained echoes of the Soviet era, despite the fact that Ukraine had been independent of Russia for over thirty years.

Eventually his friend, Max, strolled across the yard and the two teenagers fell into step with each other as they headed homewards. Normally the conversation flowed freely between the two of them, but Yurii gave short answers or shrugs today. He wasn't interested in discussing the incident in the chemistry lesson or the idiotic behaviour of one of their classmates. It was clear that he wasn't handling his break-up with Nastya well, so Max tried to get his friend talking about other things. 'Have you seen how close the bloody Russians are now?' Max asked.

Yurii grunted to acknowledge the question without engaging with it. 'I wish the hell they'd go back to Moscow,' Max continued. He followed politics and current affairs closely and was feeling very uneasy about the situation. His friend had weightier matters on his mind – teenage heartbreak.

The boys said goodbye to each other on the corner of Ozerner Street and, as they went their separate ways, called out the time they would meet up later for basketball practice. Yurii crossed the road and unlocked the door to the ground-floor flat where he lived with his mother and sister, announcing 'I'm home!' as he did so. Inside, as usual, his grandmother, Vira, was in the kitchen and was warming up the soup she'd made for him and his younger sister, Arina. He still didn't feel hungry, but he didn't want to offend his grandmother by telling her this – she always went to a lot of effort to make them something nice to eat after school. As the two siblings sat at the kitchen table eating the chicken soup, Yurii's mood improved along with his appetite. He politely answered his grandmother's questions about his day until her attention was taken by an incoming phone call, which she stepped outside the kitchen to take.

Despite his general disengagement from anything that didn't relate directly to his heartache, his attention was taken by his grandmother's lowered voice. Her whispered conversation was clearly not meant to be overheard by her grandchildren, but such secretive behaviour was so out of character that it had exactly the opposite effect. He sat up straight and strained to hear any clues. Instead of her normal, warm chattiness he sensed anxiety. He caught the word 'Putin' a few times, spoken with a venom that was unlike her.

As she finished the call and returned to the kitchen, he asked her if everything was alright. She hesitated for a moment before asking Arina to go and fill up the water bowl for her dog, Byron. Once his sister was out of the room, Vira asked her grandson if he was aware that the Russian army was right on the Ukrainian border. He said that he and Max had been talking about it but that's what the Russians did wasn't it? The Russian bear liked to stalk close to its smaller neighbour and remind them who had the power in their fraught relationship. They'd go back to Moscow soon enough. It would be fine. His grandmother smiled weakly at her grandson's optimism and started clearing the table.

Yurii heard his mother arrive home from work so called out 'hello' from his bedroom. Since her divorce from his father, she had worked longer hours at her job as an accountant and had relied on Vira to help out with the children. He could hear the two women in the kitchen talking about the Russians so he decided to leave them to it whilst he got ready for basketball. He loved the game and had the perfect physique for it; he took practices seriously and was highly competitive. In fact, he expected to succeed at anything he did, so failure brought a dark mood – just as the end of his relationship with Nastya had. Before leaving for practice he poked his head round the kitchen door, noticing that his mother looked tired and stressed, but deciding not to pass comment. He told her he was off to basketball and with that he left, slamming the front door behind him and meeting up with Max as planned.

As they walked along, kicking a ball between them, Max brought up the subject of the Russians again and this time Yurii was more responsive, 'Yeah, my grandmother is getting worked up about them too.' But then his usual positivity took over and he explained away her anxiety – her parents and grandparents had lived in Ukraine through the horrors of the Second World War so she had been brought up on stories of wartime atrocities. But that was a different time, a different generation. He retrieved the ball from the road and started bouncing it along the pavement, warming to his theme, 'Putin isn't a complete idiot! He's not going to start a war – he just wants to scare Zelensky.' Max stopped and stared at his friend, 'Why is he sending so many troops to our border? I don't like it.' As they arrived at the sports hall Yurii dribbled the ball towards the far end of the court and shot it neatly through the hoop. He turned to Max and smiled at him, 'You need to chill, mate.'

Following an energetic practice, both boys walked home together discussing the upcoming basketball match and who was likely to be on the team. The exercise had done both of them good. Yurii had stopped dwelling on his romantic break-up and Max had put the Russian question to the back of his mind. They were now more focused on their plans for the weekend: Yurii and Arina were going to meet up with their father for a cycle ride in the park by the Dnipro and then they'd get something to eat. His sister's preference was normally for sushi but he might be able to persuade them to go for a pizza instead. Since his parents had divorced, his weekends were shaped by doing something with his dad, whom Yurii loved spending time with.

Oleksandr K., known as Sasha or Oleks, was a hero to his son. Now in his late forties, but still strong and physically fit, he'd been an action man when younger and his son had been enthralled by his stories. Sasha had wanted to be a pilot like his father and his grandfather before him, but his mother had been opposed to the idea. Instead, he learned to parachute and then went on to become an instructor, clocking up more than 1,000 jumps in the process. On one occasion his parachute had failed and he described to his wide-eyed son how he bounced off the ground and broke both his legs. Undaunted, he then learned to paraglide, becoming a Ukrainian national paragliding champion. Yurii would look with wonder at the cabinet full of his father's medals and listen open-mouthed to his stories of paragliding off mountain tops in Tibet. He begged his father to let him try out the sport but, conscious of his responsibilities to his family, Sasha would not allow it. He'd had too many friends die in paragliding accidents.

Despite curtailing Yurii's dreams of gliding through the air, Sasha always had fun and exciting plans for his children. He taught his son to kitesurf on a reservoir in Kyiv and how to repair a kite, then two or three times per year they'd go to Odesa and kitesurf on the Black Sea. Once, he gave Yurii a motorbike riding lesson on an industrial estate, but the bright blue Honda Deauville was so heavy that his skinny son, then only fourteen-years-old – struggled to hold it up and it crashed over on its side, scratching the gleaming paintwork. After that Sasha paused these lessons while he rethought what he could do with his son. The solution came in the form of an electric monocycle which made them both roar with laughter as they spent an afternoon learning to ride it. Yurii was frequently a passenger on the back of his father's motorbike, even riding pillion to the Carpathian mountains on camping trips. After his divorce, Sasha built a small house for himself on the edge of Kyiv and Yurii would cycle over there and willingly help his father with the building work. His reward was to have time with the man he adored and a bonus was the BBQ that often followed.

So spending time with his dad at weekends was always a pleasure and seeing his friends had to fit around that. The boys agreed that they should meet at their favourite tech shop, Citrus, then go roller skating or to the cinema. *Spider-Man* was on but so was *No Time to Die*. They'd see if Andrii wanted to join them and then they'd vote on which film to see. Just talking about the weekend lifted his mood; he was a teenager with good friends and his mum would give him money to spend. Life was alright.

Chapter 2
Ombersley, UK – February 2022

"Rainy, flaky, heavy – yes!" There was such satisfaction in nailing Wordle in three. Two felt a bit too quick and easy and more to do with guesswork then brainwork. But any more than three goes brought about a declining sense of achievement. I shared my score with my husband, Rick, and a few friends, then opened up my Scrabble app. I always had a dozen or so games on the go and it was my turn to play on four of them. As I submitted my words I felt a particular pleasure at hitting Debbie with VALETING – bingo! I only ever managed to take about one game in four off her, whereas I was fairly evenly matched against Margie. The three of us were all English teachers with many years' experience teaching English as a foreign language and we all had a corresponding love of language. My other opponents were strangers whom I knew only by name and their Scrabble scores.

Still on my phone, I checked my email and had a quick look at social media. Very much a political animal, I had been in a state of outrage about Brexit and Boris Johnson for years. My anger could be eased by sharing articles illustrating his self-serving actions and general unfitness for office. He was currently dealing with the fallout from the Sue Gray report which exposed how parties were held in Downing Street during Covid times. Whilst most people followed the government's rules restricting the number of people who could meet up together,

Number 10 became Party Central. I felt particularly aggrieved that the most notorious of the parties had taken place on the day of my mother's funeral, which was the day before Prince Philip's. Members of my family had travelled to Worcester from London, Kent and Cornwall but could not stay with me overnight or even come back to my house after the funeral. They obeyed the rules and made return trips of several hundred miles whilst people who worked in Downing Street cracked open the booze and turned up the music. Karma was coming Johnson's way and, as far as I was concerned, it couldn't come soon enough.

Outside my bedroom window a dirty grey sky formed the backdrop to leafless trees and brown fields, like a child's picture of an English February day. Getting out of bed, I still appreciated the fact that most mornings these days I could get up when I wanted. The days of school runs were far behind me and my post-Covid life gave me a pleasant degree of choice and flexibility over how I spent my days. The main pressure to get me up and doing came from our two dogs, who I knew were waiting for me in the kitchen, staring through the glass door anticipating my appearance. Barney and Bella were never indifferent to me, they were like fervent disciples awaiting a sign from their leader. The joyous yelping and dance of excitement when they saw me couldn't have been more enthusiastic if I'd just risen from the dead.

I switched on the TV and the kettle, then gave the dogs their morning treats whilst listening to the news.

For a few days now the BBC had been reporting Russian military activity on the Ukrainian border, with satellite images showing a massive build-up of troops. Meanwhile, as if giving the 2-fingered salute to Putin, citizens of Kyiv carried on their normal activities in the city: meeting up in coffee shops, working, shopping. A few were interviewed and were dismissive of their strongman neighbour's posturing – they'd seen similar before. Looking at the images of this sophisticated European city, with its gleaming gold and green onion domes and the mighty Dnipro weaving its way towards the Black Sea, I felt regret that I'd never visited it, despite a number of business invitations and having plenty of contacts in the city.

The dogs watched me patiently, their eyes following my every move. They knew there was a very good chance that a walk or a game of ball was on the cards, but there was also the possibility of neither happening until later in the day. Although my flexible schedule brought variety to my life, it brought uncertainty to theirs. But then they exploded into excitement as 'Aunty' Jan came through the back gate and tapped at the door. This was the sign they needed – a morning walk!

As Jan clipped the dogs' leads on to their collars, I pulled on my jacket and boots. It wasn't that cold for February but the recent storms had caused flooding along the river Severn and churned up much of our usual walk. Once we got to the fields we let the dogs off to chase crows and follow scents whilst we discussed anything of note that had happened in the past twenty-four hours. We were very much on the same page politically and had spent years fuming about the behaviour of Boris Johnson and how everything he did was driven by his own self-interest; it was always Johnson first and country somewhere further down the line. Now his downfall was just a matter of time and it gave us plenty to talk about as we walked along footpaths and over the ridge with its views of the Severn Valley and the Malvern Hills. It wouldn't be long until these fields were alive with the colours and smells of rhubarb, maize, barley, rapeseed and asparagus, but right now they were fifty shades of brown.

Needing a break from the subject of appalling British politicians, we turned to the ominous activities of the Russians. I took out my phone and retrieved a meme I'd seen of a dog with an uncanny resemblance to Putin and the line *Not sure if he's gonna bark or invade Ukraine!* We laughed at this, then discussed our good fortune to live on an island that gave us a certain amount of protection from past and present European predators such as Hitler and Putin. However much we loathed the current government, we knew that we had plenty to be thankful for and that our geography protected us from foreign tanks massing on our borders. Even though the Russians were probably just sabre-rattling, it must be chilling for the Ukrainians to know what Putin could do if the mood took him.

Back from the walk, I switched on my computer ready for a video call with my Japanese student, Maki. She'd had regular English lessons with me since Covid hit in 2020. We discovered early on that we had both been a bit nervous about these lessons; although she had an advanced level of English, she lacked confidence in speaking it and I was a bit worried that she would want to focus on her work as a foreign exchange analyst. Although I was used to leading conversations on just about anything, from the cement industry to oilfield engineering, talking about finances would never get my pulse racing. As it turned out, I could help build Maki's confidence and fluency by getting her to talk about many different topics in addition to her work. She was interested in politics and current affairs, so we always had plenty to talk about; I think she enjoyed seeing me get worked up about the latest shenanigans of various MPs and ministers and she lapped up new vocabulary such as 'snake oil salesman' and 'sleaze'. She'd then explain how dreadful Japanese politicians were, though to me they all seemed very beige compared to the colour and turbulence of the British cabinet.

During my lesson with Maki, the dogs waited patiently outside the study. As soon as I'd finished, they sat up to see what I was going to do next. I was used to the pressure of being watched by the dogs, but I wasn't any good at resisting them. They would watch silently every time I opened the fridge door, their eyes following my every move. Milk from fridge to cup then back to fridge. Cheese from fridge to chopping board then back to fridge. To them it might have been like watching a game of tennis, wondering how it would end. Maybe with a morsel of whatever I was eating – hurrah! Or maybe with nothing – shame!

Any time I opened the back door, they whimpered with excitement as they imagined it was time for a game of ball or a walk. This meant that even if my plan was just to get in the car, I would often succumb to their pressure and play a quick game of ball first. Bella was absolutely obsessed and would retrieve and return the ball ready for it to be thrown again. Barnes was usually excited for the first few throws but would then lose interest and go and sniff something rather than continue the game. Back in the kitchen, I gave them a couple of treats to keep them busy whilst I was out, and headed off to Worcester.

From our village of Ombersley there is a fast, smooth A-road swooping and curving past fields and farmland before heading off to the M5 motorway, leaving the city-bound traffic to turn off for Worcester. Progress into the city was normally steady until the road reached Barbourne, at which point pedestrian crossings slowed vehicles down; as the traffic crawled along The Tything drivers had an opportunity to look at the windows of the numerous antique and independent shops. Passing the handsome buildings of the Royal Grammar School (known to locals as 'RGS') on my left always triggered fond memories, both as the place which had educated our three children but also for its role in the development of our business.

Rick and I had set up Kingsway English Centre in Worcester city centre in the early nineties after returning from three years working abroad in Indonesia and South Africa. Rick had been an engineer in the international oil industry whilst I had spent some of the time teaching English as a foreign language to adults. Once we were back in the UK we felt uninspired to work for other people so started to think about setting up our own business. Our ideas crystallised into what came to be Kingsway English Centre, an executive level service for professional people who needed to improve their English for work or pleasure.

Whilst I focused on the academic side of Kingsway, Rick took on the business side. We started by renting a couple of rooms in the centre of Worcester then, as borrowing money was easy at the time, we bought and restored a derelict house on the old city wall, Northwall House. Business was booming so when we outgrew that we bought 40 Foregate Street, later adding next door, number 41, and turned them into the perfect environment for our discerning clients. Over the next thirty or so years we honed our service to the point where Kingsway was well-known nationally and internationally and we were proud of our reputation for providing a top-quality service. We were also able to respond to demand for a junior equivalent of Kingsway by setting up Kingsway Summer School in 2013: an English language summer school for teenagers. This was based at RGS – their own excellent facilities were only 500 metres away from our adult centre and fitted our brand perfectly.

We welcomed thousands of students from all over the world, both adults and teenagers, including hundreds from Russia and Ukraine. I had been to Russia on a number of occasions to take part in marketing events and once, in St Petersburg, I had been taught the 'proper' way to drink vodka by a couple of Ukrainians. We'd had a real laugh and I'd promised to visit them in Kyiv one day. Rick and I had even hosted Russian summer school teenagers in our own home, including one who was completely unhinged but very entertaining. He came from a very well-connected family and his path into politics was mapped out for him. Listening to the news of the buildup of Russian troops made me reflect on the fact that by now he could well be moving within Putin's orbit – a terrifying thought.

Kingsway's service was centred on providing English language training but it included responsibility for airport transfers, accommodation, a social programme and welfare. Keeping all our clients, staff and other providers happy was a full-time and demanding job, and from about 2016 I was keen to reduce my hours, although this was easier said than done. When Covid hit in 2020, it was the first time in over three decades that actually reducing my hours was easy to achieve. Those students who were with us in March of that year left as soon as they could and on Friday 20 March we drank a glass of champagne with our staff and spoke about meeting up again 'on the other side'. At the time we had no idea of how long this might be but I'd probably have guessed at two or three months. Such innocence.

Covid changed everything for us as it did for so many other businesses. It slowly dawned on us that re-launching Kingsway after the pandemic would take a huge amount of time, effort and money. At this point Rick and I were in our early sixties and we didn't have the energy and enthusiasm that we'd had when we started the business. We couldn't even be sure if or when people would be ready to travel internationally again. Furthermore, we were fairly certain that video-conferencing would lead to a reduction in people who wanted to come to the UK to learn English. I felt tired just thinking about the work involved and realised that I'd had enough. Now would be as good a time as any to finally close the doors on Kingsway English Centre and so, by the autumn of 2020, it ceased to be.

Meanwhile we weren't ready to stop working altogether. Taking stock of what we had, we realised that with our lovely building on Foregate Street and our many years' experience of delivering a first-class service for professional people, we could work with the local business community. So Kingsway English Centre became Kingsway House Business Centre, offering serviced offices, meeting rooms and hot-desking. Little did we guess that, despite our new focus on local businesses, our international contacts and experience were going to become unexpectedly useful as the clouds darkened over Ukraine.

Chapter 3
Kyiv, Ukraine – February 2022

Yurii had slept well, as always, but today he woke before his alarm went off and immediately had a sense of something being seriously wrong. His mother, Nataliia, was in his room talking about explosions, telling him to get up – her panic was close to the surface. His sister was stuffing belongings into a bag. It took a few seconds for him to work out what was happening. 'Hurry up!' urged his mother, 'We're leaving now.' Still blinking away sleep, he soon discovered that he had slept through some rocket attacks: at 4 a.m. Kyiv had been rocked by explosions from cruise and ballistic missiles. Putin had done what most people thought he was unlikely to do: he had ordered his armies to invade Ukraine. Kyiv, Yurii's city, the place where he was born and had spent his whole life, was under attack.

What should he pack? How long would they be away for? Where were they going? It was guesswork for all of them and his mother's insistence that they hurry ratcheted up the tension. She was speaking rapidly on the phone, the device wedged between her ear and her shoulder whilst she emptied the kitchen cupboards of essential supplies, chivvied her children, grabbed some things for the dog and urged them all to the car. Yurii checked his phone, which had been pinging like crazy with messages from his friends and his father. Everyone was in a state of shock, not sure what to do, where to go.

From their home in the north of the city, they headed to the west of Kyiv where Grandma Svetlana lived, but the normal route was closed. The city had changed overnight and the roads were full of soldiers manning barricades. Nataliia found an alternative route, cursing under her breath. Arina held on tightly to Byron, burying her face in his fur for comfort, trying not to cry. Yurii tried to process what he was seeing and hearing. They passed the smouldering ruins of burning cars and buildings. They passed cars laden with passengers and bags and pets. The whole city seemed to be on the move – where was everyone going?

Svetlana's flat was somewhere the children had always loved to visit. She was a well-educated and cultured woman who always had time for her grandchildren, enjoying taking them to the theatre, the opera and the ballet. But today was different from any other visit. After leaving their car in the underground car park, they took the lift up to her tenth floor flat. Instead of her normal warm welcome for the children and her daughter-in-law, Svetlana looked serious and drawn and hugged them all in silence. Both women were close to tears which fuelled the children's anxiety: if the adults were scared, the situation was very bleak indeed. The wail of an air-raid siren started up and they all hurried back down to the car park. It was full of people who had been wrenched out of their old lives and into a new reality.

They made themselves as comfortable as possible in the car, looking at their phones to try and make sense of what was happening. There was a message from their president explaining (just in case there was any doubt) that the Russians had attacked the country on a number of fronts. There was information on what to do when the sirens went and which apps to download for further information and news. Outside, they could hear explosions and occasionally the ground trembled. Messages from friends across the city shared the shock of what was happening to them all. Those who had family or friends outside Ukraine started to think about the feasibility of going abroad for safety. Then the reality of martial law hit them all like a punch in the gut – men over eighteen couldn't leave. Yurii's father, Sasha, would have to stay and potentially be called up to fight.

Over the next three days all residents still living in the block automatically went to the underground car park whenever the sirens sounded and returned to their flats when they heard the all-clear. The flats were fairly new, with four reassuringly quick and reliable lifts, so the residents never had to queue. Later in the conflict the frequent power cuts meant the lifts were often out of action and Svetlana would have to climb the stairs to the tenth floor.

Although everyone was terrified about what was happening to their city, there was still mind-numbing boredom to deal with. What do you do for hours on end in an underground car park? They huddled under blankets to try and keep warm and dozed fitfully to pass the time. They talked to each other for hours, far more than they would ever do in normal life, bringing about an unusual but pleasant closeness. They messaged friends and family and felt a sense of national unity and outrage against Putin's armies. Sometimes they watched a downloaded movie whilst crammed together in the car. Yurii had Groundhog Day on his phone and the irony wasn't lost on him when he started watching it for the second time. Then came the day when Sasha came to say an emotional goodbye to them all as it was clear that they couldn't stay in Kyiv and he couldn't go with them.

The news bulletins showed a terrifying line of Russian tanks to the north of the city. The front of the line was less than 1 kilometre from the city and the back of the line was over 30 kilometres away. Yurii's home in Ozerner Street was in a northern suburb close to the main route in to central Kyiv. It was surely only a matter of hours or days before the Russian military machine would force its way along the streets of the capital. And then what?

Living in a state of emergency in Svetlana's flat was not sustainable; they needed to find a place of safety where they could live without fear until this war was over. Svetlana had a friend, a retired professor, who lived in Łódź in Poland. He had said that she, Nataliia and the children would all be welcome to stay with him in his small flat. There was only one spare bedroom but they would manage. If they found it too cramped in Łódź, the plan was for Yurii to leave and make his way to Lisbon, where friends of Sasha were heading and happy for the teenager to join them there.

It was decided that Yurii would travel to Poland by train as the long car journey with all of them, their belongings and Byron would be squashed and difficult. They would all meet up in Poland soon. When the time came for him to leave, his grandmother gave him a large amount of US dollars in cash. He tried to resist, knowing that it would be safer with money on his card rather than carrying her cash, but she clearly wanted him to take it. His mother, grandmother and sister all hugged him and cried as he left for the station in a car driven by a friend of Svetlana. His insides were churning and his heart was hammering but it felt better to be taking action rather than sitting in the car park waiting for the Russians to invade.

Kyiv-Pasazhyrskyi central railway station was heaving with people trying to escape from the capital and head for the safety of Poland. The main route west was through Lviv – a city in the west of Ukraine, about 70 kilometres from the Polish border – so this was where all passengers were heading. Whilst locating information on the departure board, Yurii overheard an elderly woman telling her son in a tremulous voice that she was afraid of travelling on her own. Yurii, too, was feeling nervous about the situation he was in and realised that he and the woman could help each other. He offered to accompany her to Lviv, which she gratefully accepted. Her son gave Yurii a smile of thanks as he hugged his mother a tearful goodbye.

The two of them joined the crush on the platform, sticking close to each other for mutual support.

Within minutes, a metallic, clattering noise got closer and louder until the train itself appeared and jolted to a halt. People surged towards it whilst the guards fired bullets in the air to try and keep order. Amidst all this chaos and noise, the crowd parted in an unbelievable act of kindness for the elderly woman and her young escort, Yurii. They each managed to get a seat whilst the train continued to fill up. Long after it was technically full, more people squeezed on. Every inch of the carriage was full with people, luggage and pets.

Relatives on the platform, mainly men, put their hands against the window panes as a final goodbye to their loved ones or made a heart shape with their fingers. The carriage was filled with the sound of sobbing, sniffing and miaowing as the train lurched forward. For a while people didn't speak. The enormity of what was happening to them and their country was overwhelming; the train was taking them away from everything and everyone they loved. They were leaving their husbands, brothers, fathers and friends behind to cope with whatever Putin's army chose to do. There was relief at getting on the train but no sense of celebration.

The normal journey time from Kyiv to Lviv was about nine hours, but the overladen train went more slowly than usual, stopping in the middle of nowhere from time to time, as if needing to take a breather before carrying on. Early on in the journey Yurii assessed his chances of getting to the toilet as zero – there was nowhere for people to move to let him, or anyone, through. If he tried, he would never get back to his seat so he decided not to drink during the journey. He texted his family to let them know he was on the train then, after a while, the small group he was sitting with began to talk to each other. They were all in a very similar situation – heading for Lviv and then to Poland. The elderly lady and Yurii had contacts in Poland to help them but the others were just going to take their chances. They all exchanged phone numbers in case they needed to share a taxi onwards from Lviv.

The sight that greeted Yurii at Lviv station was like nothing he had ever seen before. There was a vast mass of traumatised people but there was order and kindness too. People were queuing for free food, drink, blankets and information. People were everywhere: sleeping on benches, sleeping on the ground, huddled together. He gratefully accepted a bottle of water and a sandwich, then helped his elderly companion to meet up with her lift.

Then he was on his own again and keen to continue his journey to Poland. He found the bus station but the cost of a ticket to Warsaw seemed exorbitant. Even though he had his grandmother's money, it didn't cross his mind to use it. Instead, he phoned one of the people from the train carriage and before long they were re-united and discussing with a taxi driver a price for going across the border into Poland. The taxi driver was friendly and helpful and the fare was a quarter of the price of a coach ticket, but there were six of them in a space for four. Yurii's long legs were crushed against the front passenger seat and he had a girl sitting on his lap, making it difficult for him to move – it could barely get more uncomfortable. Once the taxi had crossed the border into Poland, Yurii asked the driver to stop at the next train station, which turned out to be Zamość . He would rather travel alone by train than continue in such cramped conditions.

Extricating himself from the taxi, he stretched out his aching limbs before saying goodbye to his travelling companions and they all wished each other luck. It was the early hours of the morning and other than a couple of Polish station staff, the station was deserted. They asked the teenager where he had come from and where he was going to, and were kind enough to make him a hot drink whilst he sat and watched the sky turn to pink and yellow. As the sun rose he felt an unexpected deep sense of peace.

Chapter 4
Ombersley, UK – February 2022

On 24 February 2022, I woke up as usual at about 7.30 a.m. and instinctively reached for my phone. My first reflex of the day was always to turn on the Today programme on Radio 4 and listen to the news whilst continuing to doze. But I soon snapped awake as the enormity of what was happening hit me: Russia had invaded Ukraine. Talk of tanks heading for Kyiv was both chilling and incomprehensible.

Whilst listening to the BBC account of events, I saw I had a message from Stanislav, a Russian student who had been to Kingsway several times. He was a dentist who had been improving his English in order to take exams and work internationally.

Hello dear Sue! I'm so sorry that I'm Russian. Me and all of my friends here against the war. But the gang that sits in the Kremlin does not care. I feel like a hostage.

I replied:

Hi Stanislav – we know that political leaders do not always represent their people very well. I wish the Russian people would overthrow Putin. These are difficult times, stay safe.

I turned on the TV to see images reminiscent of the Second World War: a sophisticated European capital was full of soldiers preparing to defend their city from a foreign aggressor. Not just soldiers but volunteers in civilian clothes holding guns and operating checkpoints. Even the language harked back to an earlier era – air-raid sirens, bomb shelters, tank traps, rocket attacks. I thought of my mother who, as a child, had lived in London through the Blitz and regularly spoke of the terror of the sirens; decades later the sirens in the TV comedy *Dad's Army* would stir up old fears in her. As I watched the citizens of Kyiv settle down to wait out the raid in the metro stations, I remembered her stories of going to London underground stations during air raids. We were now eighty or so years after the Nazis had inflicted terror on Europe, but the similarities were striking.

Ukrainian people in their thousands were leaving their capital city clutching children, pets and carrier bags, and dragging suitcases behind them. Some were in overloaded cars, many were crushed onto platforms at the railway stations and others were walking along roads with no apparent end. One image that stayed with me was of a mother with her young children and their grandmother in a car that had got a puncture. They were at the side of an almost empty road whilst the Russians were thought to be approaching from the other end. It was stressful and unbearable to watch but the camera moved on to other scenes of fear and misery.

The BBC map showed alarming red arrows indicating the routes of Russian troops: some were attacking from Crimea in the south, others were moving towards the eastern cities of Mariupol and Kharkiv, but the ones that had me transfixed were moving south from Belarus towards Kyiv. Two fat arrows showed how near to the capital city the Russian tanks were. I instantly thought of all the Russians I had met over the years: were any of them in this invading army? What did they think of Putin's decision to start a war? I also thought of all the Ukrainians I had met and how terrified they must be. It was hard to process what I was seeing. Why would Putin choose to bring death and terror to his own people and to an independent neighbouring country?

A BBC statistic lodged in my mind: 18,000 machine guns had been handed out to volunteers who wanted to defend their city. The thought that one minute you are a bricklayer, a teacher or an actor and the next minute you are working out how to fire a gun ready to kill invaders was mind-blowing. As Putin called on the Ukrainian military to overthrow their own government, Zelensky asked residents to prepare Molotov cocktails with which to greet the Russian invaders. Martial law was introduced on the day of the invasion meaning that men aged eighteen to sixty, with a few exceptions, were not allowed to leave the country. In an equivalent situation in the UK my own son and my daughters' partners would all be on standby for military service. How could this be happening in Europe in 2022?

The BBC journalist in his flak jacket and helmet flinched involuntarily as a rocket shrieked overhead. His commentary was breathless with shock, as he tried to describe what he was seeing and hearing. There were distant explosions, cars on fire at the side of the road and an apocalyptic feel to the scene. The film cut to President Zelensky defiantly refusing to accept an American offer to fly him out of the country and telling Putin that he and his government were staying put. Dressed in army fatigues, he looked angry and shaken but determined as he spoke to his Russian opponent to leave him in no doubt that he was a leader who intended to lead; he was not about to surrender to the Russian war machine. Zelensky, the former TV star and comedian, had bravery running through his veins and a gift for oratory that would help to give his people hope. Cometh the hour, cometh the man.

World leaders were quick to denounce the invasion. President Biden said, '*The Russian military has begun a brutal assault on the people of Ukraine without provocation, without justification, without necessity.* […] *Putin is the aggressor. Putin chose this war. And now he and his country will bear the consequences.*' He then went on to explain that a coalition of partners, including 27 members of the European Union, the UK, Canada, Japan, Australia and New Zealand would work together to impose severe sanctions on Russia. NATO forces would be strengthened and ready to protect its commitments to member states.

This was Boris Johnson's moment to look serious and Churchillian and he seized it. In a televised address, he declared that the '*hideous and barbaric venture by Vladimir Putin must end in failure*' and told Ukrainians that the UK was '*on your side*'. Then, addressing Russians, he said '*I cannot believe this is being done in your name, or that you really want the pariah status it will bring to the Putin regime.*' Johnson had shown that he could behave like a statesman when the occasion suited him and his support for Ukraine made him a hero in that country.

Rick was on reception when I arrived at Kingsway House later that morning. I showed him Stanislav's message. Aside from shaking our heads in disbelief and uttering a few expletives, it was hard to know how to react. This Russian, whom we knew so well, had woken up to find himself as potential cannon fodder for Putin's army. This Russian was educated and open-minded and keen to further his career as a dentist, yet the leader of his own country had thrown his hopes and dreams into jeopardy. This Russian was just one of millions whose lives were now in turmoil. It was frightening and it was unfair.

My mind kept returning to Kyiv and those red arrows poised over the city. I imagined myself in an equivalent scenario in the UK except I shifted my life back to a point when my daughters were still at school and my son, Tim, was at university. Neither Rick nor Tim would have been able to leave the country due to martial law, so I would have had to choose between getting myself and the girls to safety or staying to support the men. But of course at that time in my life, my parents were still alive, so would I leave them to fend for themselves or cram them into the car too? And what about our dogs? And my parents' dogs and cats? And where would we go? Who did we know outside the UK who could accommodate three adults, two teenagers and a variety of animals? Precisely no one.

In fact the reality in 2022 was that my three children were all adults and living their own lives in different parts of the UK: Tim in Cambridge, Anna in Bristol and Toni in London. Rick and I continued to live in the family home but we had four bedrooms that were empty much of the time. Yet there were people on our TV screens whose lives could be saved by our surplus space.

An idea started to form ... maybe I could throw a lifeline to a few of these people? I would rather try and fail than watch the unbearable TV pictures and do nothing. Why wouldn't we try and help?

Chapter 5
Poland – February 2022

The peace of the early morning was shattered by the arrival of the intercity train as it clattered into Zamość station then lurched and hissed to a stop. Yurii got on, found himself a seat in a half-empty carriage and sat down next to the window. After the slamming of doors had finished, there was a moment of silence before more hissing, then the train jolted off on its five-hour journey to Warsaw. He plugged his phone in to recharge and, as the intercity settled into its rhythm, he allowed himself to enjoy feeling warm and safe, and closed his eyes. Since leaving Kyiv the day before he had barely eaten or slept and there had been no opportunity to wash or to clean his teeth. Images of the past twenty-four hours flickered through his thoughts as his breathing slowed and deepened.

Slurred words jolted him awake. The unkempt man before him repeated them, 'Dobre zdrowie' and took a slug of vodka. Yurii smiled weakly, shrugged his shoulders and said, 'English.' The drunk's face came closer to the boy and he stage whispered something in Polish, his rancid breath like a malodorous cloud. The boy shrugged his shoulders again and looked out the window. Needing a more responsive audience, the man staggered down the carriage singing a tuneless song which relied on a shouted chorus followed by a few mouthfuls of vodka.

A middle-aged woman sitting nearby shook her head and rolled her eyes at Yurii as the drunk disappeared.

She addressed him in English, 'That was a good way of getting rid of him,' she said. 'Well I don't speak Polish,' he replied. 'So where are you from?' she asked. As Yurii told her his story, the woman listened in astonishment. 'You're only sixteen and you're travelling across Europe alone?' she said, shaking her head in disbelief. This was followed by her personal thoughts on Putin, which demonstrated the correct use of a wide range of derogatory expressions. She told Yurii to be very careful, then wished him luck as she got out at the next station.

The train hurtled on through the woods and forests of the Polish countryside before arriving in Lublin where it filled up with passengers heading for the capital. The next stop was Dęblin and after that there were glimpses of the waters of the mighty grey Vistula to the west as it, too, headed in the direction of Warsaw. Before long the train was clattering through the suburbs and into Wschodnia station on the east side of the city.

Yurii passed through the ticket barriers and onto the station concourse, where his eyes widened at the sight before him. He took a sharp intake of breath before letting out an elongated 'Wow!' Filling the station concourse were large welcome signs in Ukrainian, blue and yellow flags everywhere, tables with food, drink and blankets, information stands in Ukrainian and volunteers in high vis jackets. Although there were vast numbers of displaced people looking tired and lost, the Poles were doing everything to make them feel welcome, supported and cared for.

He hadn't eaten since Lviv station the night before and his last drink had been at Zamość station that morning. Helping himself to the food and drink on offer, he started talking to a young volunteer in a bright yellow jacket. He found out that her name was Vika; she was Ukrainian but had moved to Warsaw for work some years before. He asked her how he could get to Portugal, to which she laughed and replied, 'That is not a normal question!' but said she would try and find out. He felt a connection with this young woman who spoke his language and made him feel less alone.

His father's words kept echoing in his head: 'If it doesn't work out in Poland, find your way to Lisbon.' There he could hook up with some of his father's friends, who were planning on finding somewhere to live in the Portuguese capital, and stay with them until the war was over. These friends were currently driving from Kyiv to Lisbon but had broken down in France so

Yurii had time to consider his options, one of which included the possibility that his family and the professor would have enough room to live together and there would be no need to leave. If he had to leave then he would need to find his way to Portugal.

He decided to take a train out to the airport and investigate flights to Lisbon, having heard that some airlines were offering free flights to Ukrainians. Not only were there no free flights but the only tickets available were very expensive. Despite having his grandmother's cash on him, he felt that this situation did not warrant using it. If he decided to go to Portugal, he would travel overland by coach or take advantage of the free train journeys that most European countries were offering to Ukrainians. He'd have to pay for a coach but it would be direct whereas travelling by train would be complicated but without charge.

Not sure what to do next, he returned to the station in Warsaw. By this time it was evening and he was beginning to feel an anxiety, verging on panic, something he had never felt before. His heart was hammering, he hadn't slept properly for two days and he was alone in a foreign capital whilst his country was under attack. As darkness fell, he smiled with relief at spotting Vika and asked if they could go together to get something to eat and drink. She agreed and he immediately felt his breathing and heart rate slow down.

After they'd eaten, Vika told him that she needed a cigarette and wouldn't be long. But rather than sitting at the table on his own, he followed her into the smoking room – being near her was comforting, as if she was his big sister. Yurii watched her take a deep drag of her cigarette and he felt her looking at him intently as she exhaled. Although he had eaten well today, he felt depleted and ill, and being naturally skinny meant he didn't have an ounce of fat on him to keep the February cold at bay. He didn't need a mirror to know that his face reflected the lack of sleep and stress of the past few days. In answer to Vika's question as to where he would sleep that night, he put on his usual act of bravado and said that he would find somewhere at the station, he would be fine. In response she immediately took out her phone and had a quick, muttered conversation with someone before telling him, 'I can't leave you to sleep outside on your own tonight. It's freezing cold and you're only sixteen! My Ukrainian friend Marta can put you up.' Yurii closed his eyes for a moment and let out a long, deep sigh as he whispered his thanks and, using the directions on his phone, headed off to find Marta's apartment, his life in a small rucksack on his back. He'd be warm and safe tonight and see Vika again tomorrow.

Chapter 6
Ombersley, UK – March 2022

As Russian missiles landed in Kyiv, a terrifying 48-kilometre-long column of tanks squatted to the north of the city. In the east, tanks lumbered towards towns and cities with names that were soon to become familiar from war reports: Luhansk, Donetsk, Kharkiv, Zaporizhzhia and Kherson. Much of the terrified populace in these areas uprooted itself to try and find safety, while the British public could only look on with a sense of horror and helplessness. These awful images, like something out of a Second World War film, showed clearly where this conflict was heading. There were widespread calls from the British public for the government to open its doors to those fleeing Putin's war machine.

Finally, three weeks after the Russian invasion, on 14 March 2022, Michael Gove MP stood up in the House of Commons and acknowledged the growing pressure for the UK to react to the plight of desperate refugees, '…. the unfailingly compassionate British public want to help further. That is why today we are answering that call with the announcement of a new sponsorship scheme, Homes for Ukraine……… Our country has a long and proud history of supporting the most vulnerable during their darkest hour. We took in refugees fleeing Hitler's Germany, those fleeing repression in Idi Amin's Uganda, and those who fled the atrocities of the Balkan wars …….'

The new scheme was a generous and imaginative answer to the problem of accommodating large numbers of people fleeing Ukraine. It enabled sponsors to host refugees in their own homes in return for a small 'thank you payment'. Within hours of the Homes for Ukraine website going live it had crashed but, by the end of the first day, more than 100,000 Brits had managed to register.

Whilst many British people were desperate to help these desperate people, the Home Secretary of the day was in no such hurry; Priti Patel was exactly the wrong person to lead the response to a humanitarian crisis. As one of the cheerleaders of Brexit, and with a well-deserved reputation for smirking nastiness, she was wedded to the idea of 'getting control of our borders'. This meant that, even as we witnessed heartbreaking scenes of terrified people trying to get to a place of safety, the Home Office was insisting that refugees would have to demonstrate that they earned enough money or had skills that benefited the UK. Brexit meant Brexit. Patel was short in stature and she was equally short of empathy and humanity.

Exhausted and distressed Ukrainians were given endless bureaucratic hurdles to overcome: lengthy forms to fill in, documents to scan and upload, identities to prove, distant visa centres to attend. It was assumed that these people had left their homes in an orderly manner, remembering to bring with them all their important documents and having a smart-phone that was fully charged and connected to Wi-Fi. Within two weeks of the launch of the Homes for Ukraine scheme there had been 28,300 applications but less than 10% (2,700) had been granted a visa. The Home Office was accused of heartlessness and foot-dragging even by the government's own MPs.

One major problem with the Homes for Ukraine scheme was that the potential host had to have named Ukrainian(s) to sponsor. Not only was this not made explicit on the website, but it seemed unrealistic that significant numbers of British people would know Ukrainians that they could sponsor. Many Brits signed up to the scheme then waited to hear who they had been matched with. Some waited months hoping for news but heard nothing. They would wait indefinitely as the aim of the site was to collect data about potential hosts and where they lived so that local authorities could prepare resources for possible demand. It was the government's failure to create its own system for matching refugees to sponsors that meant people like me, with Ukrainian connections, were asked for advice and help by both Brits and Ukrainians.

The day after Gove announced the new visa scheme, I was contacted by a Ukrainian doctor, Alla, whom I had known for some years. She was a qualified and experienced paediatric neurologist who had taken a number of English courses at Kingsway to prepare for a medical exam; without this language qualification she couldn't work in her professional capacity in the UK. Alla was now living near Worcester and working in a local hospital but her family and friends were still in her home city of Odesa on the southern coast of Ukraine. She wrote to me on Messenger and attached some documents:

'Hi Sue - Today I started to fill out forms according to the new rules for my sister with 2 children 9 and 12 years old. I also help my friends, these are 3 of my colleagues. For the updated form they need a sponsor. Could you help me find sponsors?'

I replied that I would do my best but the information she had sent me was hard to decipher and I couldn't tell what related to whom. It was all a bit of a mess but if she could come in to Kingsway, I'd try and sort it all out.

We met up that afternoon and I listened to Alla as she gave me details of her family and friends who lived in the south of Ukraine. Her parents had a farm in Odesa and had no intention of leaving it. Her sister, Polina, wanted to come to the UK with her two young daughters. Alla also had a number of friends and colleagues from hospitals in Odesa looking to escape to safety. Watching her chew on her lip, her face tense and drawn, was so different from the positive and smiley woman that I had got to know. She was putting a lot of faith in me to help these people.

As she provided me with more information, I wrote notes and asked questions and linked these to the passport scans she had provided for each person so that I had a coherent outline for each of them. I then sent an email to 4 local people who knew I had connections to Ukraine and had already told me they wanted to help. The information I had was sketchy:

Mother and 2 daughters:

Polina (born 1980)
Anna (born 2010)
Kateryna (born 2013)

Single female

Olga aged 43. Currently working as a radiologist in Odesa.

Single female & daughter

Nataliia and 6 year-old daughter Marta. Was working as a radiologist in Odesa but has already escaped to Poland.

Married female

Kateryna is a paediatric dentist. She was on holiday in Sri Lanka when the war broke out. She will stay there until she finds a place to go. Her husband is with her but intends to return to Ukraine to join the war effort.

This was my first attempt to match people so would be an indicator of whether potential hosts would step up with such limited information. The response was positive and immediate with all four of my local contacts ready to share their homes. I looked at the accommodation they could each offer and allocated the refugees accordingly. Within a few hours of promising to do what I could, I was able to tell Alla that I had found sponsors for everyone in her group. It seemed too easy. Having matched sponsors to Ukrainians, I gave each side the other's contact details and the link to the visa application site. Between them they had to plough their way through pages and pages of questions about the applicant and the host and they had to upload documents on to the system. This process effectively shut out anyone who didn't have a smartphone or whose documents had disappeared in bombed homes or workplaces.

The scheme, designed to help refugees reach the safety of the UK, had no sense of urgency; it was more like an obstacle course to stop people coming here. This must have suited the Home Office as they could point to the scheme as evidence of our 'culture defining hospitality' at the same time as making it as difficult as possible for anyone to actually get here. On television we watched the scenes in Poland and neighbouring countries as millions of people arrived from Ukraine exhausted and desperate. They were made welcome by the Polish people and international volunteers despite the overwhelming numbers.

In contrast to the open-armed and practical approach of Poland, Britain's response was mired in bureaucracy of its own making. There were plenty of official statements about the new Homes for Ukraine scheme and boasts that there would be no cap on numbers. But only a trickle of people were actually arriving in the UK. As criticism of Britain's response mounted, the Home Office announced that there would be a 'surge team' in Calais to support people wanting to come to Britain, so a small number of refugees made their way to the French port. On arrival, bone-tired and emotionally numb after days of travelling, they were sent from building to building to look for this Home Office support. Eventually they found three men at a trestle table in a deserted departure hall. They were given water, crisps and chocolate and told to go to Paris or Brussels to sort out the necessary paperwork. The next available appointments were in a week or so. It was like a marathon runner crossing the finishing line and being told that actually they had to run another marathon to complete the race.

The generosity of the British people was being squandered by a government who put control of immigration above saving human lives. It was shameful.

Chapter 7
Poland – March 2022

Yurii opened his eyes and blinked several times, taking in his surroundings. Outside the traffic noise suggested that it was morning and, checking his phone, he saw that it was 11.00. The books, toys and cartoon duvet cover clearly indicated that he had been asleep in a child's room. He was warm and comfortable and had slept for about twelve hours. He was also in a foreign country about 800 km from home.

He yawned and stretched whilst he remembered the events of the previous few days. He'd travelled from Kyiv to Warsaw by train and had met Vika, who was a volunteer at the station, helping those arriving from Ukraine. It was thanks to her that he'd had a bed last night, in her friend Marta's apartment.

As he opened the bedroom door he heard a radio playing so called out 'hello!' followed by 'pryvit!' when he remembered that his host was Ukrainian. Marta called back that she was in the kitchen and to come on through. They'd had the briefest of conversations when he'd arrived the previous night – she'd shown him the bed and he'd crashed out within seconds.

Whilst Marta boiled some eggs to eat with sourdough and cheese, she asked about his journey and his family before her tone of voice became harsh and aggressive as she made it clear what she thought about Putin. Then her phone pinged as a message from Vika arrived inviting them both over to her apartment.

Meeting up with Vika again was as comfortable as seeing an old friend, yet they'd only met the day before. Her apartment was full of boxes and packing cases as she explained to Yurii that she'd only just moved in and still hadn't finished unpacking. Today she was a bit more organised so could offer him a bed and, as his mother, sister and grandmother would be in Warsaw in about a week, he would be welcome to stay until then. She warned him that the only cooking appliance she had was a sandwich toaster so they would need to be inventive with meals. But they'd manage.

In the following days Yurii borrowed Vika's bike and cycled around Warsaw familiarising himself with the city. There was the Vistula river again, dividing the city into right and left bank, with the gleaming glass office blocks of international companies towering above it. He loved the Old Town and Castle Square in front of the royal castle with its outdoor cafes and street entertainers and Sigismund's Column in the middle. Getting off his bike at the Palace of Culture and Science, he read the plaque stating that this had been a gift from Stalin. Who wants gifts from murderers? he wondered. He knew enough about Stalin to know that he and Putin were two of a kind.

As he cycled around Warsaw's tourist routes and landmarks, he began to feel an affinity with the city. He felt at home here and the sight of Ukrainian flags everywhere was uplifting. He saw the similarities between Warsaw and Kyiv and understood how they had both endured unbelievable horrors during the Second World War, caught between the 20th century dictators, Hitler and Stalin. And now his country was in an existential war with the 21st century dictator, Putin. If Ukraine did not manage to boot the Russians out, then Poland would be in a very vulnerable position yet again.

On March 12th, a week or so after Yurii had arrived in Poland, his mother texted to say they had arrived in Lodz so he should join them as soon as possible. It was a two-hour train journey west to reach the city and on arrival he made his way to the apartment where they were all staying. It belonged to a retired professor from Lodz university, a friend of his grandmother who had generously invited them all to stay. There were two bedrooms, one of which was the professor's. The second bedroom was taken by his mother and grandmother, his sister slept on a makeshift bed in the dining room and Yurii on a makeshift bed in the lounge. And of course Byron the beagle was with them too. Cramped was an understatement but they were all safe and they were grateful.

Every morning Yurii and Arina had to fold up their beds and create space so that the five of them could move around. After breakfast they would all go for a walk along the main thoroughfare in Lodz, Piotrkowska Street. At around four kilometres long, its wide variety of shops, cafes and monuments provided plenty to occupy them and they could easily spend a whole day wandering from Liberty Square to

Independence Square before returning to the flat for dinner. During the day they would shop for ingredients for their evening meal and the professor clapped his hands with delight when Grandma Svetlana made zurek for them all – a traditional Polish soup. Yurii could tell that the professor enjoyed their company but he also sensed that he didn't expect Yurii to stay. Several times he asked about Yurii's onward journey to Lisbon and the others discussed this too as if it was just a question of time.

If he left, then the others would have more room and he might end up somewhere nice in Lisbon. He drew on his characteristic positivity to imagine that the weather would be better and there might be a beach nearby. Leaving Kyiv on his own had been extremely difficult – not just leaving his family and his city whilst it was under attack, but not knowing how he would manage until his mother arrived in Poland. Leaving Lodz after only 3 days was so much easier, even though everyone was crying as he got into the professor's car to get a lift to the station.

His plan was to go west to Berlin and then head south, but there were no trains leaving that day. Instead he tried to get a coach, but was told that he couldn't buy a ticket as he was under age: children could not leave Poland unaccompanied. Eventually he was allowed on a coach which appeared to be going to Berlin, but actually went to a large refugee camp outside Warsaw. He was given a wristband and instructions as to where to head for in the camp. His stomach churned and his pulse raced – what was happening? This was not the plan! Making a quick decision he got back on the coach and returned to the station in Warsaw. By this point it was very late and he hadn't made much progress since leaving Lodz. He checked Google maps again and decided to head for Prague in the morning. The station was quiet and there was no sign of Vika so he resigned himself to spending the night on a bench. Scared that someone might steal his rucksack with all his possessions, he hugged it to his chest and waited for morning.

The first train to Prague was full and, despite the time of day, there were lots of drunk people. But, unlike the drunk passenger on his journey to Warsaw, these people were friendly and wanted Yurii to have a drink with them. He declined politely but when they handed him a beer, it seemed better to accept than risk causing offence. He put it in his rucksack then closed his eyes. These people were boisterous but he felt safe with them.

The journey to Prague took about eight hours during which time he had nothing to eat or drink. Arriving at the main central station, Praha hlavní, he smiled and muttered 'tak!' at the sight of the refreshments available for refugees. After satisfying his hunger, he took the opportunity to have a wash in the station toilets then made his way to a stationary train carriage which was designated as a sleeping space for refugees. Talking to others who were resting there, everyone expressed surprise that he was travelling alone. There were adults travelling alone or with another adult and mothers with young children and/or teenagers. But he was the only lone teenager.

He slept fitfully during the night and became aware of a man crying in the darkness, lamenting the death of a relative. There wasn't much anyone could do to ease the man's pain but Yurii gave him the can of beer as an act of sympathy.

The next morning he travelled from Prague to Munich which turned out to be the final place where he was welcomed with food, drink and help. There he was surprised to be told that there were no direct trains to his next destination, Lyons. He checked this information on his app and with the ticket office. To get to Lyons he was advised to go to Stuttgart and then through Switzerland, changing four times en route. He would need to keep awake and alert or he'd miss a key connection.

Chapter 8
Ombersley, UK – March 2022

As soon as the British government's Homes for Ukraine visa scheme was announced, I decided to get in touch with all our business contacts in eastern Europe and offer to try and help any Ukrainians who wanted to come to the UK. I could work out the next step if anyone took me up on the offer. And of course Rick and I would be prepared to host too. On the 15th March 2022, using our newsletter software, we sent the following email to over 5,000 of our Kingsway English Centre contacts:

Dear XXX

Ukrainian Crisis

It's hard to believe that only a few weeks ago Ukraine was a peaceful and thriving European country. But following Putin's invasion, we have all seen scenes of suffering, terror and destruction that are reminiscent of the second world war. As millions of Ukrainians flee their homeland, it is up to the rest of Europe to step up and offer sanctuary.

The British government has been very slow to set up a system to help Ukrainian refugees, but they are now encouraging British people to sponsor named individuals and welcome them into their homes. There is still some paperwork to complete to get a visa but, from March 18th, this can be done much more easily (apparently) online. We'll see.

LEAVING UKRAINE

I am writing to everyone in our database of students including Russians as we know that a lot of Russian people are disgusted at Putin's violence and lies. The reason for doing so is to spread the word that, using our old Kingsway contacts, we are trying to match Ukrainian refugees with people in the Worcester area who want to provide accommodation. If you are Ukrainian or have Ukrainian friends or family please forward this email to them. There are plenty of Worcester people who want to help but they don't have a personal connection to a Ukrainian person. By forwarding this message, you may help us reach people in need. Anyone who wants a home in the Worcester area should reply directly to me and we'll decide how to proceed

These are dark times and it is up to all of us to do what we can to help those whose lives have been devastated. The peaceful world order will return if good people do the right thing.

In response to my message 31 people unsubscribed from our newsletter including 8 Russian addresses. I was most surprised at a Russian language travel agent whom I'd met in the UK and Russia on a number of occasions over the years and had a good relationship with. He had been educated in the USA and spoke excellent English:

Hi Sue,
Just to let you know that most people here support Putin. I personally support him 100% and all people who I know support him. Your understanding of the situation is based on the news that you get

from BBC and CNN, we are getting completely different news here and most people tend to believe them. It wouldn't make any sense to get into argument as the picture that we have in our heads is so different. The reason I am writing you is to let you know that by taking side and sending out such letters to Russian agents you will find little support if any and turn most Russian agents against you.

However, such negative responses were in a minority. More common were such as these:

Dear Sue!
Thank you for your letter and offer
Of course I do it
I hate Putin
(Russian)

Dear Sue,
Thank you for your letter and for the understanding that Russians are deeply disgusted at everything our government is doing. We are in real shock and feel guilt and shame. We are so sorry but we can't do much. We are doing what we can but it isn't enough unfortunately. I'm sorry to say that I don't know anyone from Ukraine who flee to the uk. I have friends who are now in Germany. But if I find out anybody who is in the uk I will definitely give them your contact. Offering a shelter for these people is a great job Sue. You are kind and honorable people. Thank you.
(Russian)

LEAVING UKRAINE

Dear Sue

Thank you very much for your kind email. I do have relatives and many friends in Ukraine who are for the moment in safe place in the country or already in Poland or Italy. But I will pass your offer to them in case there are some other refugees who are still in need.

And thank you for your understanding towards Russians who do not support the violence. I can say from myself and from all the team of XXXXXXXXX that we are as devastated by the recent events in Ukraine as the whole civilised world. We absolutely disapprove of the decision of our government and condemn the invasion.

We hope very much that this atrocity will be stopped very soon, though the deep shame for Russian attack, I'm afraid, will stay with us forever.
(Russian)

Dear Sue,

Thank you very much for your e-mail, for support and understand in what a terrible situation is around us in Europe. This is caused by one person. He is not a human one. He is a terrorist. His propaganda is so powerful for Russian people, that they believe in Putin, but not Ukraine and even not their own children or relatives... This is disaster. But Ukraine will win. We will win.

After the general responses to my message came a steadily growing number of people asking for help and sponsorship to get to the UK. One of the first emails from Ukraine asking for help made my heart pound and I held my breath involuntarily as I read it:

Dear Sue
My name is Andriy xxxxxx. I am currently fighting for my Ukraine as a captain of the Armed Forces of Ukraine. Arthur xxxxxx gave me your coordinates. My wife and our two sons, who are one month old, would like to seek asylum in the UK. It is important to me that they stay away from hostilities. If there is an opportunity to provide some shelter, I will be grateful. If possible, please write what documents or actions are required of her.
Sincerely grateful
Andriy xxxxx
P S We will win 100%.

This man had the most unbelievable stress in his life – he was fighting on the front line for his country whilst worrying about the safety of his wife and newborn twins. Subsequent emails explained that he was trying to organise his family's evacuation as his wife didn't speak English and had her hands full with the babies. As if he didn't have enough problems in his life, he warned me that he often couldn't get phone signal or Wi-Fi to reply to emails.

Having a baby is a massive event in anyone's life, even if you are living in ideal conditions. Having newborn twins when your country finds itself at war and your husband is called up to fight is impossible to imagine. Then making the decision to leave your home and friends to try and get to a country where you don't speak the language, have never been and have no contacts is off the scale in terms of trauma.

Despite the gravity of her situation, I thought that the chances of finding a British person willing to accommodate a woman with no English and newborn twins was remote. But if I didn't try, I wouldn't know. I asked Andriy to supply further details including names, ages, passport scans and photographs. No one would be able to travel without a passport, so this became one of my key requirements when trying to help someone. It would also prove that they were Ukrainian and, therefore, eligible for the Homes for Ukraine scheme. The other details would help them come to life and might touch a chord with potential hosts.

I had many years' experience of matching students to host families, and I had a database of Kingsway's former host families in Worcester that I considered contacting. But I hesitated. This was a completely different situation. It would be unfair to ask our ex-host families to take on traumatised refugees for an indefinite period. I wasn't sure if there would be any payment from the local authority for doing this and I couldn't be responsible either way. And as Kingsway English Centre no longer existed, these people would not be leaving home every day to study English or join our social programme. They would be at home needing the help and support of their hosts. I had to look elsewhere for potential hosts or sponsors.

So I decided to seek the help of LinkedIn to appeal for British hosts. At the time I was connected to over 1,000 people and if any of those people shared my post, its visibility would grow exponentially. I copied and pasted a flag of Ukraine and posted it online with the following:

Using my international contacts, I have become an unofficial matching agency for Ukrainian refugees. I have a growing list of Ukrainians desperate for sponsors so I am asking anyone who is able and willing to offer accommodation to contact me. It doesn't matter where you live in the UK. You just need to have the space and a desire to help people whose lives have been devastated by war. Then of course we need the new visa scheme to work ....

My post was seen by more than 4,000 people & about 100 people responded to it. Some just clicked on the thumbs up emoji or wrote words of support, others shared the post or contacted me with offers of help. I posted the same request for help on Facebook and had a wave of support from there too.

So at the same time as scores of Ukrainians were responding to my email asking for help, scores of Brits were responding to my LinkedIn posts offering their homes. The messages also came via Facebook, WhatsApp, texts and emails. I seemed to have lots of Ukrainians with the same first name and an unusually high number of would-be British hosts called Fiona. The situation was chaotic and overwhelming and I was getting very confused. I needed to come up with a system or I wouldn't be able to help anyone.

In fact it was my younger daughter, Toni, who stepped up to sort out the mess I was in. She was home from London for the weekend and could see that I needed help. I told her the information I needed from Ukrainians and the information I needed from hosts (names and ages of host family, location, rooms available, pets etc) in order to try and match them. She created a spreadsheet and helped bring order out of chaos. From this point it was just a question of filling in the columns with the key information and remembering to transfer details as they were supplied.

It was in these early days that I started struggling with the word 'refugee'. Yes it was an accurate word for people fleeing conflict and seeking refuge, but it was a loaded expression. It sounded demeaning and belittling to call people refugees and one professional woman whom I helped told me of her shock when she was asked if she was a refugee. When she realised that she was indeed a refugee in the UK, it was like a slap around the face and left her breathless. The English language is so rich with vocabulary but I couldn't find a suitable word to replace refugee. Later I found that some people referred to their Ukrainians as 'guests' or 'visitors' or even 'housemates' but none of those felt right. And at what point do people stop being refugees? Once they are settled in a home here, are they still refugees?

In fact I met very few of the Ukrainians or their British hosts in real life that I had matched up but there were a few exceptions. Ania was one of the exceptions. She had had an unpromising start in life in her home city of Kryvyi Rih in central Ukraine; her parents were poor and the city was full of drugs, crime and mafia. Yet whilst still a teenager she co-founded a cultural centre which included a theatre studio, a recording studio and a football pitch. She and her friends tracked down grants and funding for their project which enabled local people to use their facilities free of charge. Then later, after getting a degree in English, she also set up her own language school.

When she was 25 years old Ania was invited to act as an interpreter for a group of American missionaries who used to visit Ukraine twice per year. With them she went to local orphanages and got to know a teenage girl called Alina. Over time they built a strong relationship and Ania became the constant and reliable adult in the young girl's life. The relationship was strong enough for Ania to adopt her even though there was only an age gap of twelve years between the two of them. Compassionate and entrepreneurial were just two of many positive words to describe the remarkable Ania.

With desperately bad timing, war broke out a few days after she had invested all her savings in a new building for her business. As the Russians advanced, her friends urged her to leave Ukraine with them. For a few days she resisted – she had just lost all her savings and, although Alina was now an independent adult, Ania's elderly parents were frail and dependent on her. But finally she was persuaded to join a convoy of cars leaving the country via Slovakia to head for Switzerland. The first blow to their plan came when the young men in the group were prevented from crossing the border due to martial law, and only Ania and a female friend were allowed through. As if the trauma of leaving their families and homeland wasn't enough, the two young women then had a serious car accident in Austria and their car was written off.

Despite the obstacles, they did eventually get to Switzerland and Ania found herself staying with friends of friends in a French-speaking area. Having no money, she immediately started looking for teaching work, emailing her CV to schools in Geneva and surrounding areas. She got very few replies but occasionally she was given some feedback such as the fact that business hadn't picked up post-Covid or that she needed to speak French to stand a chance of finding work.

One day she felt a glimmer of hope when Garry, director and owner of The Language House in Geneva, replied to her email to suggest a Zoom call. During the call he told her that she had an impressive CV but that her lack of French made it difficult to offer her any teaching. Sensing her disappointment he told her that she would be better off going to the UK. The British government had introduced a visa scheme to help Ukrainians and he had a contact in the UK who was trying to help. He typed my email address into the chat box and said, *'Write to Sue and explain your situation. Good luck!'*

Ania felt an affinity with the UK although she had never been there. Teaching English was her life so getting to the home of the language would be like a dream come true and, as she wasn't having much luck finding a job in Switzerland, she decided to test the water with the UK. She wrote to me immediately but braced herself for disappointment; either I wouldn't reply or wouldn't be able to help her. In fact I replied within hours to say that I could and would help her. In her reply she said, *'I don't think I can thank you enough. I was literally crying when I received your email. I didn't believe it was possible and still don't believe it. Thank you! Thank you so much.'* I quickly matched Ania to Eileen and Mike, a very sociable and hospitable couple who lived in my village. They had a lovely home in the centre of Ombersley and their 3 children were grown up and living elsewhere. Eileen was a retired English teacher and was keen to offer a home to a Ukrainian refugee – it was a perfect match. I gave them the link to the Homes for Ukraine scheme then left them to proceed with the visa application whilst I got on with trying to make other matches.

It was some weeks after this that the UK had its first ever Platinum Jubilee bank holiday to celebrate 70 years of the Queen's reign. My token effort towards the celebrations was to make a Platinum Jubilee trifle, the royal themed dessert which had won a national competition. It was a lot of fiddly work, but looked very impressive with its layers of lemon and mandarin crowned with white chocolate jewelled shards. My kids were home for the weekend and we'd just finished our royal feast when the doorbell rang. At the door was a young woman who checked that I was Sue Johns and, when I confirmed this, she burst into tears. I knew it was Ania before she told me. We both hugged and, although she just wanted to give me a bottle of wine and a thank you card, I persuaded her to come in and meet the family. She then made a lovely speech about how lucky and grateful she was to be in our country and how wonderful British people were. She was overwhelmed by the kindness of people in general but bus drivers in particular; it was unbelievable that you could stay seated until the bus had come to a complete stop! No need to stagger along the aisle whilst the bus was still travelling – so civilised! And she was amazed that such facilities as public toilets existed. No need to limit drinking when away from one's home! And the fields all look so tidy and cared for! And British people valued and preserved old things rather than chasing after the new. The list was extensive and humbling. Things we took for granted or moaned about were appreciated by those who didn't have them. It was good to see our country through another's eyes and to be reminded that, despite some of our politicians and problems, we were fortunate to live in such a place.

From time to time over the next few years Ania and I would meet up at social events or go for a drink or coffee together. She was good company and we always had a laugh and at some point, invariably, an exchange something like this:

Ania: 'One day they will make a film about you.'

Me: 'I know – film directors are already pestering me. It's annoying.'

Ania: 'Yes I can imagine. Who do they want to play you?'

Me: 'Emma Thompson. She'll do I suppose. I'm not sure who they've lined up to play you.'

Ania: 'Kate Winslet?'

Me: 'I'll check. If not, leave it with me. I'm owed a few favours.'

Ania: 'Thank you. It's good doing business with you. Who will play Yurii?'

Me: 'I think he'll want to play himself. Oh and I think it will be set in Hollywood.'

Ania: 'Of course. Ombersley is just too English.'

Ania's English was so good that she was able to introduce me to a phrase I had never heard before - pay it forward. It means repaying kindness and help received by doing the same for others when you get the chance, rather than paying back to the original good Samaritan. She did exactly that by helping and translating for the local Ukrainian community, getting involved with village activities and eventually working for the local housing department.

Ania is one of life's do-ers and givers and I know that one day she will return to Ukraine and help her country get back on its feet. That will be absolutely the right thing to do but she will be badly missed here.

Chapter 9
Germany and Switzerland – March 2022

Plonking himself in a window seat, Yurii stared at the passing views as the train left Munich. Raindrops on the glass blurred the view but the outskirts of the Bavarian capital were drab and unremarkable. The train gathered speed as it headed towards Stuttgart. Yurii allowed his eyes to close but didn't dare fall asleep; he needed his wits about him for changing trains. A kaleidoscope of images tumbled through his mind: tanks in Kyiv; the overcrowded train which took him from his home city; the taxi in Poland which he got out of as he could barely breathe; Vika helping him in Warsaw; meeting up with his family in Lodz; washing in station toilets; filling up with food where he could; sleeping in a stationary train carriage in Prague. Only three weeks ago, at this time on a Tuesday, he would have been in a chemistry lesson or messing around at lunch time with Max or Andrii. That was his world before Putin's invasion. He knew his friends had also left Ukraine but they were with their mothers and were heading to Austria and Germany. He wondered about his teachers, particularly the male ones – they might even be in the army now. He felt anger and sadness at how one man's actions had upended the only world he had ever known.

When he next opened his eyes he saw that the carriage had filled up with commuters on their way home. People were now closing their laptops and unplugging their phones, packing their things away as the train eased into Stuttgart. He shrugged on his jacket and checked his rail app for one final time before leaving the train. There was plenty of time to find the correct platform for the next leg which was to Karlsruhe. His phone told him that this German city was very close to the French border and the river Rhine. If nothing else, his journey was a lesson in European geography! In Karlsruhe he located the platform for his next train and before long he was on another train collapsing into another seat, letting out a long sigh as he did so. His eyes struggled to stay open but he couldn't risk falling asleep as he would have to change trains again after crossing in to Switzerland in less than two hours' time.

Arriving at Basel SBB railway station, he scanned the departure board and saw that he had about 15 minutes to get to platform 32. That gave him enough time to call at a station shop and pick up a bottle of water and some bananas. He had been travelling for about 12 hours with nothing to eat or drink since Munich. It was about 9 pm now and dark; he was cold, tired and hungry but he had no plan other than to push on towards Lyons. This involved travelling right across Switzerland and changing trains a few more times. His train arrived bang on time. He boarded and took a swig of water as it pulled away from Basel. He had to stay awake.

A short time after leaving Basel the train suddenly jolted to a stop. He peered out the window into the darkness but there was no clue there. Probably traffic lights. The other passengers carried on doing what they were doing; nothing unusual going on here. The inter-carriage doors opened with a whoosh and a uniformed man made his way down the aisle talking to the passengers as he went. There was a ripple of laughter which accompanied him. Whatever he was saying was making people laugh but, as he was speaking French, Yurii had no idea what he was saying.

He caught the eye of the young man sitting opposite him and asked him in English what the conductor was saying. Shaking his head and smiling, the man answered in English with a French accent, 'He says the train driver has disappeared and he's asking if any of the passengers know how to drive a train!' Yurii responded with a laugh and they both joked about why the driver had run away. They soon fell into an easy conversation and before long Yurii had told the story in a matter-of-fact way of his journey from Kyiv and his aim to reach Lisbon. He'd never met his father's friends and they had nowhere to live yet but they'd work something out. Maybe he'd just spend some time on the beach until the war was over. It would be fine. Yurii was used to the reaction he saw in his fellow passenger's eyes as he related his journey. He always faced the same questions about why he didn't stay in Poland and why his mum allowed him to head off alone and how he felt about going to a country he'd never been to live with strangers. The war had led everyone to make difficult decisions and he'd just got on with it. No fuss. No drama.

The train lurched forward and the teenager made a joke about who might be driving it now – maybe someone who wasn't actually qualified as a driver? The young man, Mathieu, laughed and offered him some chocolate. 'So where are you staying tonight?' he asked as the boy accepted the chocolate and shrugged his shoulders, 'on a train, I suppose or maybe at Geneva station.' Yurii saw the flicker of shock in the man's eyes so smiled back at him to show that it really wasn't such a big deal. But Mathieu's next words were unexpected, 'Well you can sleep on my sofa tonight if you like?' He felt his jaw drop before he uttered the words, 'Really? Wow that would be fantastic! Thank you.' Yurii trusted his newfound companion and was relieved that he would have somewhere safe to sleep that night.

Later the teenager found out why Mathieu had offered to put him up overnight. Their conversation had revealed that Yurii was only sixteen rather than the university student that he'd initially assumed him to be. He was travelling alone in very distressing circumstances and didn't speak either of Switzerland's main languages: French or German. Once he realised that Yurii was considering sleeping overnight in Geneva station, Mathieu's instincts as a former policeman kicked in. He had had plenty of experience dealing with drug addicts and low life who could potentially target the young boy. He'd also been on the receiving end of kindness himself during his own travels in Australia and now it was his turn to a help young person in need.

The two of them changed trains in Lausanne where there was enough time for Mathieu to treat the teenager to a hamburger. Yurii was thrilled and grateful and quickly devoured the burger before the final leg of their journey. It was nearly midnight as the train came to a halt in Rolle station on the edge of Lake Geneva. Mathieu led the way out of the station and Yurii followed, grateful that someone else was making the decisions for once. They both zipped up their jackets and pulled up their hoods against the cold mountain air. Mathieu said something in French into his phone before sighing and turning to Yurii, 'Thanks to that idiot train driver, we're going to have to walk. I can't get a taxi and it's too late to call anyone for a favour. Sorry.'

The walk from Rolle to the little village of Gilly where Mathieu lived took nearly an hour along silent, rural roads edged by vineyards and lit by stars rather than streetlights. Not a single vehicle passed them. Yurii kept up his usual level of friendly chat and positivity despite the long walk, the cold and the rain. He was grateful for the company and the fresh air was a welcome change from spending so much time in train carriages. His departure from Prague had been seventeen hours ago and he must have travelled about 800 kilometres since then. He discovered that Mathieu was on his way home from Bucharest but, although that was a journey of 3,000 kilometres, it was only a few hours by plane.

They were both relieved when they finally reached the warmth and comfort of Mathieu's flat. It was just after 1 am when Yurii crashed fully clothed onto the sofa and fell instantly asleep.

Chapter 10
Ombersley, Worcestershire UK
March – April 2022

'Dear Sue, I beg you, please, we are searching for a safe place and family who can accept us. My name is Anna, I'm fourteen years old. Also I want to rescue my mother, Olena. We like cooking Ukrainian food, love speaking, and my mom is a Ukrainian designer. We live in Kyiv and now we're here. I can speak English fluently, looking for education. I do ballet 5 years and learn IT technologies, learning franish, german. My dad is in the army. Protects Ukraine from Russia. We stay to support him but now the situation is bad, so we need to evacuate ourselves. We are tired of not sleeping, sitting in the bomb shelter. We are looking for chance to stay in UK and continue our life in safe place I will be very grateful to you! Thank you so much!'

As I stared at the email on the screen, my heart pounded, my blood ran cold and I held my breath involuntarily. This young girl had reached out to me from a bomb shelter in a war zone. To me, a stranger, 2,000 miles away. She should be going to ballet lessons and having fun with her friends not trying to find a safe place where she wouldn't live in constant danger of being killed. I tried to imagine my own daughter, also called Anna, in a similar situation as a young teenager, writing an email in a foreign language begging a stranger in a foreign country to help her and her mother. Me. Tears of sadness and rage pricked behind my eyes. I immediately sent two emails, one to Anna saying I would help her and one to a Worcester woman called Karen who had just contacted me to offer her spare room.

I then set off for my business networking group which was usually an upbeat affair as it signalled the end of the working week. The final part of the meeting involved each member giving a brief summary of what they'd been up to business-wise and there was normally plenty of banter and good humour. Whilst waiting my turn to speak, I gazed out of the windows on the second floor of Sixways Stadium. Beyond the car parks and sports centre, there were rugby pitches, rolling fields with horses and sheep and the distant hills of Malvern and Abberley. All these places were ordinary and safe. Everyone deserves ordinary and safe but I kept thinking of Anna in the bomb shelter who would have to leave her own country in order to find somewhere ordinary and safe. Every few minutes the room was filled with laughter or cheering.

Then it was my turn. 'Tell us what you've been up to Sue,' said the group leader with a big smile on his face. 'I'm sorry but I'm about to drag the mood down,' I replied as twenty five pairs of eyes turned to look at me – some apprehensively. This wasn't a normal thing to say at the end of our networking meetings, but I couldn't be flippant when my mind was filled with an image of a young girl and her mother hiding in a bomb shelter. I read out Anna's email. The room was silent. 'Dealing with requests for help like this is taking up most of my time at the moment,' I offered as my reason for not being active business-wise. There is nothing really appropriate to say in response to an email like that. There was a lot of shaking of heads and murmuring of sympathy and support in the room, so I asked people to spread the word that I needed to find homes for more people like Anna.

After the meeting I returned home to find that Karen had already replied saying that she had cried when she read Anna's email and of course she would sponsor her and her mother, Olena, to come to the UK. Within a few hours of receiving Anna's SOS, I was able to reply to her and say that I had a sponsor for her and that she could apply to come to the UK under the Homes for Ukraine scheme. Karen was so concerned for the safety of the mother and daughter that she told them to leave Kyiv as soon as possible and she arranged for them to stay with some friends of hers in Poland whilst waiting for their visas. She was later successful in getting the independent King's School in Worcester to give Anna a free place and she helped Olena to find work. The transformation in Anna's life came down to a chain of people, each doing their bit:

I had emailed my European network offering to try and help;

People in my network had forwarded the email until it reached Anna;

Anna had written a compelling email to me;

A local friend had told Karen about my efforts;

Karen had contacted me and followed through with a prompt and generous offer of help.

Finding a suitable host family so quickly for Anna and her mother was encouraging for me and potentially life-saving for them. All I was doing was writing emails but by connecting the right people I was helping Ukrainians find safety and that was its own reward. I had another early success with finding a home for Andriy's wife, Alla, and their newborn twins. Andriy was one of the first Ukrainians to ask for my help; he was in the military and had been desperate to find a safe place for his family. I hadn't been hopeful that anyone would want to take on a woman who didn't speak English and had two very young babies. However, a retired health worker called Linda, from Warwickshire, rose to the challenge. This case needed more paperwork than usual as the twins had to get passports and Andriy had to try and organise this and the visa applications whilst on active service. However they did eventually get to the UK and, in due course, I was delighted to receive the following update from Linda:

Hi Sue
Just to let you know that Alla and the twins are settling in well. She is lovely the boys are gorgeous and I think she is the perfect guest. Although Alla spoke no English on arrival I am amazed at how quickly she is learning. Thank heavens for Google translate!!

In fact the amazing Linda later sponsored Alla's mother to join them, so she had three generations of the same family living with her and she told me that she found the experience very rewarding.

The tricky cases kept coming. When Ruslana emailed me to ask for help, I shook my head in despair at her situation. She was a 33 year old teacher who was 20 weeks pregnant with her first child and her husband was away fighting. Taking on a pregnant woman would probably involve being her birth partner too so I wasn't hopeful that anyone would want this role. But, checking my lists, I found Sue who lived near Weymouth and had young grandchildren and all the equipment necessary for when they came to stay. In her email to me Sue had stated that she could host a pregnant woman or a mother with a young child. I emailed her with details of Ruslana's situation and she didn't hesitate. After a Zoom call they both wanted to proceed with the visa application and Ruslana was in Dorset before too long. Although they lived happily together for several months, I was surprised to hear that Ruslana had decided to go back to Ukraine to have the baby. This was partly due to homesickness and partly wanting to be near her mum and husband. She was given permission to fly at 37 weeks and gave birth to a full-term, healthy baby girl by C-section.

Those looking for accommodation in the UK were, unsurprisingly, mainly women and many were travelling with their children. There were single women travelling alone but also family groups which could include very young children and/or teenagers and/or grandparents. Sometimes there were dogs or cats in the group and occasionally there was a man who was of military call up age. I knew there were exemptions to conscription for medical reasons, for men over 60 or for men with three or more children. Students with a place to study abroad were also allowed to leave. Finding out the reason why a man was able to leave Ukraine was part of building up an accurate picture of people seeking a home in the UK.

During March 2022 the number of Brits who contacted me offering to host under the Homes for Ukraine scheme outnumbered the Ukrainians who had asked for my help. These numbers were reversed within a couple of months but at this point, unbelievably, I had to manage the expectations of hosts who were desperate to do their bit and take in a refugee. Many of the potential hosts were empty nesters with spare rooms or people with large homes or with self-contained granny annexes. But there were plenty of people living in more modest accommodation. There were also groups of people living near each other in the same town or village who all wanted to get involved and, between them, offered to support two or three generations of families.

After a while I developed a system to maximise the chances of making a successful match between potential hosts and refugees. Rather than working with the sketchy information I had with my first four matches, I made sure I had more details about each side plus I asked this crucial question of the Ukrainians, 'Do you want to go to a specific area of the UK or are you happy to go anywhere?' If they answered that they wanted to go to a particular area (probably because they had friends or family there), then I could save myself time and trouble trying to match them to a different place. And for those who were open about where they lived, I asked them to look up a particular area on Google if I had a potential match there. Before going any further they might need to be aware for example that Cornwall is not near London. I did not share contact details between the hosts and the refugees until I was quite sure that each side understood as much as possible about the other.

Before sharing the contact details, I told them that the next step should be to make a list of questions to ask each other during a Zoom call. For example the host might be strictly anti-smoking and want to find out whether their potential house guest was a smoker or they might want to ask them about Covid vaccinations or if they had a driving licence. The refugee might have a fear of dogs and want to know about any pets in the household or if there was public transport to the nearest town. It would be better to establish such basics before agreeing to live with each other. Most people decided during the Zoom call that they wanted to go ahead with the sponsorship, but I made it clear in advance that there was no pressure on either side to commit to the other by the end of the call. It was a big decision for both sides so time to reflect was fine and, if necessary, I was prepared to be involved to deliver bad news. In fact there were very few matches that didn't proceed to the next stage: the visa application.

The government website stated that it aimed to process visa applications within three weeks, a time frame that was no more than an aspiration and unmatched by reality. The Home Secretary and other government ministers were wheeled out to apologise for the long delays. The Shadow Home Secretary called the visa numbers, 'scandalous and shameful' and the Refugee Council accused the government of, 'choosing control over compassion'. But in due course visas were issued to 'my' people and I was able to update my ever-growing spreadsheet by putting a tick in the 'Visa granted' column and eventually a date in the 'Arrival in UK' column. But, in the meantime, it was encouraging to see that, thanks to my efforts, on paper at least, little communities of Ukrainians were growing in different parts of the UK. In addition to my own home county of Worcestershire, there were clusters in Warwickshire, Gloucestershire, Devon and Cornwall and outlying hosts in Cambridgeshire, Leamington Spa, Weston-super-Mare, Hertford and London.

Strangers contacted me to offer their homes but so did family and friends. My sister-in-law, Fran, lives in the pretty little Cornish village of Flushing, across the water from Falmouth. She stepped up to the plate and gave a home to a young university student, Lina, despite the fact that she had her own ongoing health issues to deal with. Fran's family and friends rallied round to support both Fran and her young guest. Lina's new life in the village of less than 700 people was a world away from Kyiv where she had been at university until Putin's invasion. There she was one of a population of about 3.5 million and had all the facilities and attractions of a capital city at her feet. But now, rather than catching the metro to meet up with her friends in central Kyiv, she was catching the little passenger ferry across the Penryn river to the Royal Cornwall Yacht Club to work behind the bar. Local people were friendly and supportive and invited her to all kinds of things but she missed people of her own age and culture. Playing her guitar lifted her mood sometimes but it wasn't until her mother arrived to live with a family in Falmouth that she found some of her old sparkle. The Ukrainian Support Group and Ukrainian Soul restaurant, both in Falmouth, helped her to settle in to her new life until in due course she went to study graphic design at Salford University.

The Barker family were exceptional in that three family members with three different homes all took in one or more refugees. I knew Margie from the English language teaching world and, prior to the pandemic, we would meet up at international marketing events for our industry. The first proper conversation I remember having with her was in St Petersburg at a time when all Russians we met were friends or colleagues and all were very keen to send their clients to the UK on English language courses. Post-pandemic Margie and I stayed in contact through playing online Scrabble or having a coffee together if I was in her neck of the woods.

Margie's school was in the centre of the charming and historic market town of Totnes in south Devon. She was used to working with and hosting foreign students so it was a natural step for her to offer to be a sponsor under the new visa scheme. Not only did she take on a mother and her teenage daughter and give them three months of English lessons at her school, but she gave them places on the summer trips and excursions too. Margie's daughter, who also lived in Totnes, took in a young woman and that woman's cousin stayed with Margie's son in London. The two Ukrainian cousins were living several hundred miles from each other but were connected by the Barker family and they would all meet up in Totnes on family occasions.

My matching system seemed to be working well although I was conscious that the supply of British hosts was diminishing. Within a few months the situation had flipped from a shortage of Ukrainians to a shortage of hosts and it was becoming harder to respond positively to requests for help. As people reached out to me in desperation I had to manage their expectations whilst trying to find more host families.

Chapter 11
Switzerland – March 2022

Kitchen noises woke him up; the sounds of cutlery against crockery, the bubbling and clicking of the coffee machine, the whoosh of the water system, cupboard doors opening and closing. Yurii blinked and took in his surroundings. He was fully dressed and lying on a sofa in someone's living room. He looked at his phone, 8.00 am, and remembered that he was in the home of someone he'd met on a train just outside Basel the day before. 'You awake yet? Sorry!' said a disembodied voice 'but I've got to go to work. Couldn't leave you asleep! Do you want some breakfast?' Yurii realized that he was very hungry so got up, stretched and went to join Mathieu in the kitchen. 'Help yourself,' he said pointing to bread rolls, jam, cheese and coffee. As Yurii tucked into the food, Mathieu introduced him to his flatmate's American Staffordshire Terrier, Rosco, who was sniffing at the teenager's ankles.

'I might be able to get you a lift to Lisbon,' said Mathieu between gulps of coffee. Yurii looked at him wide-eyed & his jaw fell open. 'I've posted details of your situation in a local Facebook group, it seems there are some people heading from here to Lisbon soon.'

'Wow that would be brilliant!' the teenager responded.

'Look, make yourself at home and we'll talk later. Hopefully I'll have more details when I get home this evening.'

And with that he was out of the door, taking a bite of croissant as he left.

A lift to Lisbon would be incredible! He felt that the stars had aligned for him – a chance encounter on a train had led to a bed for the night and a potential lift of nearly 2,000 km to his destination! Mathieu had been generous and trusting in his hospitality - here Yurii was alone in his new friend's home: safe, warm and comfortable. He knew his parents would want to hear that all was well so he updated them via Telegram then had a long shower. His journey so far had been eased by the kindness of strangers such as Mathieu and, without their help, things could have been very different.

Deciding to take the dog for a walk, Yurii clipped a lead on Rosco and left the warmth of the house feeling the chill of the March air. His arrival in Gilly in the darkness last night had hidden the beauty of his surroundings; now he could see the awesome grandeur of the snow-capped Jura mountains and the vast grey expanse of Lake Geneva dotted with small boats and fringed with the silhouettes of houses and trees. He knew they'd passed vineyards on their walk from the station, but now he could see fields upon fields of neatly tied brown vines stretching away into the distance. Gilly was just a tiny rural village and he'd got the measure of it within half an hour or so – there was a simple white church and a primary school as well as a few shops and a fountain. There was also a nice looking restaurant, Auberge de Gilly, where he was standing trying to decipher the French dishes on the blackboard menu when his father, Sasha, rang.

He moved to a nearby wall to sit down and concentrate on the call. It must be something important or his father would have sent a message on Telegram. Without wasting any time on pleasantries, Sasha launched straight in, '*I think you should head for the UK,*' he said. '*My friend Olena P. says the British government has a new scheme for Ukrainians. It will be better for you.*' This was a surprising change of plan. Yurii agreed that it might be better, especially as he could speak English, but that he had probably got a lift to Lisbon. His father ignored the information about a potential lift, '*You will need a sponsor from the UK to get a visa so Olena is going to find someone for you.*' They finished the call and Yurii headed back to Mathieu's, digesting his father's words on the way.

He made himself a cup of tea and had just sat down to join an online conversation with his friends when he was interrupted by an incoming unknown number from the UK. He answered the call and a friendly, male voice checked that he was Yurii K. and then introduced himself as David Meddows. He explained that he ran an international summer school for teenagers in the UK and that he worked closely with Olena P., his father's friend. She sent Ukrainian teenagers to his school every summer and now she was asking for his help in getting Yurii and another boy into the UK under the new visa scheme. David checked a few details with the teenager and said he would do his best to help. Yurii thanked him and then went online to see what he could find out about the British visa scheme. Things seemed to be moving fast.

It was at this point that Yurii's life and mine converged as David and I had known each other for many years. Originally he had worked for me as a teacher at Kingsway English Centre; later he had gone on to set up his own school with his partner Claire. We used to bump into each other at international marketing events, the last time had been in Malaga just before the pandemic hit. We had sat in the sunshine having a beer between appointments, little realizing that that was one of the last normal things we would do before Covid changed everything.

David had seen my LinkedIn posts so called to tell me about Yurii and see if I could help him. I took a few notes as he was speaking, told him to pass on my phone number and said I'd do my best. Soon after I received this email:

'I've just spoken with Yurii again and he is travelling overland on the way to the UK. Sister and mother in Poland, which, from watching Newsnight *last night, is absolutely overrun. Father, who works in IT, driving ambulances in Kyiv. First impression as you would expect: charming young man, B2*, independent, largely able to look after himself. Will fit into a host family seamlessly. He will call you.'*

(*B2 = a measure of language ability indicating an upper intermediate level)

Within minutes of reading David's email I had a call from Yurii which gave me goosebumps. Seeing the war on television was one thing. Talking to someone who had just escaped from those scenes was another. He spoke English well and sounded bright, polite and confident. I found myself spontaneously offering to sponsor him to come to the UK even though I hadn't planned to and I hadn't even discussed it with Rick. But it seemed the right thing to do in the circumstances and he seemed happy and grateful for my offer. He then mentioned that he was heading for Lisbon. This totally confused me,

'What? Lisbon? Why are you going there?'

'I have a lift there and I have friends there.'

I told him that it didn't make sense to me – it wasn't on the way to the UK, look at a map! He needed to apply for a visa to come to the UK, so I asked him to promise me that he would stay in the safety of Switzerland and deal with the paperwork for coming to the UK rather than head off on a mammoth journey in the wrong direction with strangers. Mathieu too was concerned about Yurii's plans to go to Portugal and, during a subsequent three-way phone call, we all agreed that it made more sense for him to come directly to the UK. At that point I assumed the British government was fast-tracking visas for Ukrainians, and I wrongly thought that Yurii's status as an unaccompanied child might expedite the process further.

Mathieu agreed to Yurii staying whilst waiting for his UK visa, and he was kind enough to make sure he had something to do every day. One day the teenager borrowed snowshoes and went up in to the mountains with Mathieu's father; another day he played basketball. He worked hard for a few days helping one of Mathieu's friends with his landscaping business – getting up early, enjoying the physical work and even taking control of a mini-digger. He went to dinner with local Ukrainians who expressed concern that he was travelling alone, but he shrugged off their worries in his usual way. Some evenings he went to a bar with Mathieu and his friends to be sociable, not to drink alcohol; whatever was suggested, he did.

So the days passed quite pleasantly but it felt surreal – he felt like he was in limbo living someone else's life. Later, looking back on that time, he wished he'd known that everything would turn out alright but, at that point, the future was a huge question mark. He didn't even know which country he would be living in. The photos of that time seem to show a boy having fun but inside he felt anxious and nervous. Some evenings were difficult and sadness would settle on him, like a heavy blanket, weighing him down. But after a night's sleep he woke up feeling optimistic about the future.

However, the days were ticking by and the plan to go to the UK seemed stuck. He was travelling on an expired passport and the Homes for Ukraine system wouldn't allow him to complete his visa application with it; he had to renew it first. This involved an appointment at the Ukrainian Embassy and a day trip to Geneva where, after queuing for some time to speak to an official, he was told to go the embassy in Berne – nearly 200 km away. So another appointment on another day in another embassy in another city and another official hand wrote an extension in his passport. That passport had expired several years earlier and the photo was of his 10-year-old self. Not exactly what a well-travelled, independent 16-year-old wanted to show the authorities.

By the time he submitted his visa application it was March 23rd and he'd been at Mathieu's for eight days. In the best of circumstances it would take at least two weeks from submission for his visa to be issued. He was beginning to feel awkward. The small two-bedroom flat was home to Mathieu, his flatmate and a dog plus Yurii using the living room as his bedroom. Although happy for Yurii to stay, Matthieu knew that the teenager was in limbo; he needed a proper home and to go to school. His spontaneous offer of a bed for the night had turned into something he hadn't bargained for and he began to wonder whether the British visa would ever be granted.

I could tell from Yurii's daily texts that he was regretting not taking the lift to Lisbon and was losing confidence in the UK's new visa system. He wanted Mathieu to have his space back. One night had turned into over a week already so I knew I had to move him on from Switzerland and closer to the UK. I needed a plan.

Chapter 12
Switzerland to Paris
March – April 2022

Not only did I need a plan but I needed it fast; Mathieu's hospitality had been stretched to the limits and there was no visa on the horizon. My first thought was Geneviève and the Carlas. Although the name sounds like a punk band, they were in fact three women who were all friends and lived in Claye-Souilly, a small town on the north-eastern outskirts of Paris. All three were English teachers but Geneviève was French whereas the two Carlas were both Dutch, both married to Frenchmen and both had a surname beginning with 'C'. Calling them the Carlas was a lazy but affectionate shorthand to talk about them in the plural.

I had known all three for years. Our relationship had started via Kingsway English Centre when Carla Couasnon was researching a school for her husband, Bertrand. He was a beginner in English, and she wanted to be sure he was in an appropriate place for a middle-aged professional person and that the teaching focused on communication and pronunciation rather than grammar. She made a shortlist of three schools and, after several calls with me, she was satisfied that she had found the right environment for him. Bertrand came to us for about three months and made great progress.

During and following Bertrand's course, I made links with some of his and Carla's friends and we organised regular social and linguistic visits between our families and friends. My friend Liz and I had found kindred spirits in Geneviève and the Carlas; we were all of a similar age and into language learning and teaching. The "French" trio were anglophiles and keen to immerse themselves in an English environment whenever the opportunity arose. Liz and I had been on many French courses in France but had reached the stage where we just wanted to mix with French people and speak the language rather than go on a course and study it. Some of the teenagers in our families were also involved in the visits; both my daughters stayed with Geneviève during their French A level courses and the son of Carla Chazottes, Sven, came to Kingsway Summer School for two years running.

I felt hopeful that Geneviève or one of the Carlas would look after Yurii whilst he was waiting for his visa. On 23rd March I messaged Carla Chazottes with a brief outline of the situation; she was active on social media so the chances of getting a quick reply were good and speed was of the essence. She replied within minutes, asked a few more questions and told me to leave it with her. The next day, 24th March, she said that she would be happy for Yurii to stay with her and that her husband and son were fine with it too. He could arrive as soon as he wanted. This was brilliant news; I knew that Yurii would be thrilled and Mathieu would be relieved.

Eleven days after their chance encounter on a train outside Basel, Mathieu dropped his young guest at the station and waved him off on the next stage of his journey. The superfast train from Geneva to Paris ate up the 500 km as it hurtled north & Yurii took a photo of the speed as it flashed up on an electronic screen – 300 km/hour! After days of hanging around waiting for something to happen, things were now happening at speed, and not just the journey. The excitement of entering France for the first time was mixed up with the excitement of connecting with his new host family and getting a bit closer to his ultimate destination. During the journey he exchanged Whatsapp messages and photos with Carla so that they could recognise each other.

As the train from Geneva pulled in to Gare de Lyon and disgorged its passengers, Carla, her husband and son were waiting on the station concourse. They all narrowed their eyes and peered into the crowd to try and identify Yurii and, despite the hundreds of hurrying travellers and commuters, he was easy to spot. At over 6 foot tall, a lanky teenager on his own carrying a rucksack and a Ukrainian flag, he walked towards them with a big smile on his face. As they introduced themselves to each other, kissed and hugged, he felt in safe hands. Once again the relief of handing over decision-making to others washed over him.

Within minutes they were in the car, pulling away from the Gare de Lyon and crossing the inky blackness of the Seine to the Left Bank. The family seemed to be competing with each other to point out key landmarks: 'On the left, Les Invalides', 'On the right Notre-Dame!', 'Over there is the Louvre!', 'Musée d'Orsay on the left!', 'Eiffel Tower on left!'

Yurii felt overwhelmed at what he was seeing and hearing: he was being driven through one of the world's great capital cities with people he had only just met. All the names sounded exotic and magical but not all of them were familiar - Panthéon? Pont Neuf?

They re-crossed the Seine and negotiated the traffic around the Arc de Triomphe before seeing some of the same sights from the Right Bank. On reaching the historic and fashionable Marais district, they parked up and went into a busy little restaurant where they sat down at a table for four. Yurii had had nothing to eat since leaving Mathieu's flat that morning, but the strangeness of his situation inhibited him from eating much, despite being urged to choose whatever he wanted. It struck him that the restaurant was very loud with people chatting and laughing whereas the few proper restaurants he'd been to in Kyiv were, in his memory, much quieter and more formal.

As the family drove back to Claye-Souilly, they continued to chatter and point out places of interest, *'Centre Pompidou!'*, *'Place de la Bastille!'* but Yurii gave up the fight to keep awake and let his eyes close. The next thing he knew the car had stopped and he had arrived at his latest accommodation: the Chazottes' home in rue de Madrid. After eleven nights sleeping on Mathieu's sofa in a bachelor pad, he was open-mouthed with delight at being shown his room: it was a beautiful light room in the roof with a double bed and a private bathroom. And it smelt of flowers rather than his own putrid socks! He fell into bed and into a deep sleep.

Another morning, another country, another stranger's home. He was getting used to this. It was mid-morning before he went downstairs and found Serge in the kitchen with pains au chocolat and fresh bread for his breakfast. As if that wasn't fabulous enough, he was introduced to the delights of putting sprinkles onto bread and butter. Being in a large comfortable home with this lovely, friendly family put him in a happy mood. What a great place to live whilst waiting for his UK visa!

His days soon settled into a rhythm which included regular online lessons, on his phone, to finish his Ukrainian school courses. These lessons were all very early in the morning and it was a drag getting up in time, but he couldn't and wouldn't miss them. He could easily have claimed that he had problems with his internet connection or other technical issues but he was self-disciplined and conscientious and had kept up with his school work since leaving Kyiv. Putin might have disrupted his life in the short term but he wasn't going to take away his future. The lessons were important as there was a big end-of-school exam coming up in the summer and his future required him to get good grades for university, war or no war. His classmates were scattered throughout Europe but he saw them all regularly online in lessons and at other times in chat groups. They were all with their mothers or other family members but he felt a sense of pride and independence that he was managing on his own.

On the days when he didn't have to get up early for lessons, he slept in late. He was often alone during the day, but always found something to do. Sometimes he would go for a walk through Claye or be invited to join Carla's students in an English lesson. Other times he would play around on the skateboard that Sven had given him. He even enrolled on an online HR course as he liked the idea of working with people. On one memorable day Carla took him into Paris and they went to the Louvre and saw the Mona Lisa. Several times he used his grandmother's recipe and spent a few hours making borscht for the family meal.

The best part of the day was the evening when everyone was together for dinner. Eating en famille was a new experience for him and he loved it. He loved the food and he loved the sociability. He also appreciated the fact that they all spoke English when together so that he didn't feel excluded. And after dinner he loved playing Timeline with them – guessing the chronological order of different inventions and discoveries was both educational and fun. They were all speaking English as a foreign language whilst learning and laughing together.

On a daily basis he texted me to find out if there was any news about his visa. As the days turned into weeks I could only tell him that I was doing everything possible but there was no visa yet.

Chapter 13
Ombersley, Worcestershire UK
March – April 2022

The woman from the council, perched on the edge of my kitchen sofa, pursed her lips and looked sceptically at my windows, 'Do they open? I need to be sure there is adequate ventilation in here.' I proved to her that they did and gave a smug smile as if I'd just played a clever chess move and it was now her turn. 'I'll need to check the measurements of the bedroom,' she said looking at her checklist. I led her upstairs to the double bedroom with en-suite bathroom where Yurii would stay. She asked me to hold one end of the tape measure whilst she stretched the other across the length of the room, scribbled something on her checklist then peered into the en-suite, maybe to see if it was piled high with stolen goods. I half expected her to sit on the bed and declare it insufficiently comfortable. Then she said she'd like to take a quick look in the garden. 'That's a trip hazard,' she said pointing at a slightly uneven paving stone. I bit back the temptation to say that maybe Yurii would be safer staying in a war zone. 'Oh one more thing,' she added, 'Could you show me the other bedrooms?' 'But he will definitely stay in the one I've just shown you,' I replied. 'Well believe it or not some people use their spare bedrooms to grow cannabis,' she said in a tone suggesting that she'd seen it all. Presumably I would be an unsuitable person to host a war refugee if I had a few mood enhancing plants in my bedroom.

Of course I understood that the local council had to inspect the homes of people who had offered to host Ukrainian refugees. But instead of creating a fast, simple, light touch inspection they appeared to be using one designed for an altogether different type of situation. It was as if I wanted to host the Queen of Sheba and the council needed to cover themselves against being sued for inadequately regal accommodation. In addition to the home visit, I had to send in a certificate to show our boiler had been serviced regularly and a video of our fire alarm working. The clunky and onerous council inspection was a perfect fit for the Homes for Ukraine scheme: both were overly bureaucratic and both lost sight of the fact that real people in real danger were waiting for them to finish ticking their boxes.

The system was grinding slowly on with no sign of urgency. The local people who were sponsoring Alla's group of friends were jumping through the same hoops as me and we frequently updated each other on the latest bureaucracy we had to deal with. Some of us already had current Enhanced DBS certificates but we had to get another one, even those who were not hosting children, not just for ourselves but for any other adults in our household. The visa applications were somewhere in the system, but they may have fallen down the back of the filing cabinet for all we knew; neither the Ukrainians nor their British sponsors had heard anything back and the weeks were ticking by.

Being naturally optimistic I decided to proceed as if Yurii would eventually get to us, so on 31st March I wrote to John Pitt, the headmaster of RGS, to see if the school might consider offering him a free place. I was delighted with Mr Pitt's friendly and positive response. Although he made no promises, he said that once Yurii was in the UK, he would like to arrange for him to meet the various heads of department in his subject areas so that they could assess his suitability for joining the sixth form. Mr Pitt and the Admissions Team would also want to interview him informally to be assured that his English was good enough to cope with the rigours of A levels and to feel for themselves that RGS would be the right place for him. The fast and supportive response of the school demonstrated an understanding and empathy that was completely lacking at government and council level.

Meanwhile Brian and Deirdre Grainger, who used to host for us in the days of Kingsway English Centre, had sponsored one of Alla's group, a radiologist from Odesa called Olga. She was amongst the very first Ukrainians I had matched up – all of whom were somewhere in the visa system. Whilst Olga was anxiously awaiting news of her visa, Brian and Deirdre were watching the news with growing concern; Russian bombs and missiles were landing in Odesa with increasing frequency. The Graingers spoke to Olga regularly trying to be as positive and reassuring as possible but, as their relationship with the young woman grew, so did their fears for her safety. They made an appointment to see Robin Walker, the MP for Worcester, to ask for his help in expediting her visa and they invited me to come along to the meeting.

I had little respect for the government of the time, but I recognised that there were Conservative MPs who were cut from a better quality of cloth. Robin Walker was one of those MPs: a decent man with a long and strong connection to Worcester, he had helped us in the past with visa issues for Kingsway students and with business issues during Covid. He seemed genuinely interested in hearing our experiences with the Homes for Ukraine scheme and promised to do what he could to speed up visas for Olga and Yurii. After our meeting his assistants kept pressure on the Home Office and kept us informed although they were up against the same black hole of information as the rest of us.

As news of what I was trying to do for refugees spread within Ombersley, a couple of local friends came to see me to discuss how the village could prepare for potential arrivals. Their focus was on ensuring that local services and facilities could cope, so I feared more box-ticking exercises. Being in direct contact with people trying to escape a war zone meant that my priorities were completely different; getting people out of Ukraine at speed was more important to me than the impact on local services. 'We need to scoop people off the beaches before seeing if there are places at the local dentist!' I said trying to appeal to their Dunkirk spirit. I knew I was being dramatic but I also knew that people's lives were in real danger. I intended to carry on doing what I was doing in my way, but it made sense to join forces with the village group as we were all on the same side.

So on 5th April I went along to the first meeting of SUN (Support Ukraine Network) which took place in St Andrew's church. Literally in the church as there was no church hall as such. We sat in an area called the narthex at the back of the pews, opposite the altar, surrounded by hymn books and bibles. There's always an element of the Vicar of Dibley to meetings in churches or schools, so I was pleased that the organisers kept things brisk and focused. There were about 25 of us in attendance and we were all given the opportunity to introduce ourselves and say what we were already doing or would like to do to help refugees. A couple of people there were already involved in the Homes for Ukraine scheme through me and a few others were keen for me to try and match them with someone. Others did not want to host but offered to provide 'holiday cover' so that those who were hosting could have a break when required. That was a brilliant idea. Another group of people put their names down for giving lifts; this would be useful as there was no bus service at all to the nearest town of Droitwich and the 303 to Worcester had its limitations. We discussed other useful services to help people settle in such as giving English lessons, accompanying newcomers to the GP or bank or helping with job finding. After this first meeting there were regular meetings of SUN; I was impressed with the practical support on offer and the fact that a small village like ours was preparing a big welcome for any Ukrainians who managed to get through the visa system.

Chapter 14
Ombersley, Worcestershire UK – April 2022

I'd propped my mobile phone on my desk and shut the dogs out of the study whilst I waited for the call; BBC Radio Hereford and Worcester were going to interview me and I was on standby. The dogs didn't care that I was about to be heard by tens of thousands of listeners and kicked off with a cacophony of barking as a delivery driver passed our house. My stress level spiked but returned to normal as the dogs went back to snoozing.

A researcher called to say that I would hear Toni Macdonald introduce me after the next track and then I would be live. The radio host asked me fairly obvious questions about why I'd got involved and what I was doing but I made sure that my answers highlighted the gross inefficiency of the Homes for Ukraine scheme. I wanted the listeners to know that the government was full of empty rhetoric and meaningless slogans. Yes there had been a very generous response with setting up the Homes for Ukraine scheme, but it wasn't working. There were British hosts with homes ready and waiting; there were desperate Ukrainians waiting for visas; in between there was the Home Office mired in its own bureaucracy.

Either it was a coincidence or maybe the radio interview unlocked something somewhere as, later that day, I was contacted by MP Robin Walker's office asking me to provide letters from both of Yurii's parents giving their permission for him to come to the UK. I imagined that this might take a few days but hadn't bargained for a teenager + technology + impatience = super speedy response. Within hours I was in possession of letters from Yurii's parents – his mother wrote in Ukrainian and his father in English. I submitted the letters and two days later was told they had been accepted. Maybe the process was nearing its conclusion?

My own travails with Yurii's visa were just a sideshow to the main feature: my trying to help others through the process. I was regularly on the government website checking something or other when, one day, I noticed that a new piece of information had appeared. Chills ran through me and I held my breath as I read and re-read the sentence: unaccompanied teenagers were not eligible for the Homes for Ukraine scheme. The government had moved the goalposts!

I decided to ignore this information and continue as if I hadn't read it. I didn't want to alarm Yurii and I didn't want to put Carla in the position of having to decide to keep him indefinitely or send him back to Poland to rejoin his mum. Anyway, why would the authorities ask for permission from his parents if he wasn't allowed to come here alone? The answer to that was anyone's guess and didn't prove anything, although it did give me a weapon to fight with if it came to it.

Whilst I was mulling over my next step, another problem was looming. Back in the days when it was thought inconceivable that war would ever return to Europe, we had booked a family holiday in Swanage over Easter. All five of us plus the dogs were going to stay in a lighthouse on the coast path and we were all looking forward to it. But what if Yurii's visa arrived whilst we were away? Carla had originally expected to have him for a few days and he'd now been with her nearly four weeks. How could I tell her that I was on holiday so to hang on to him for a bit longer? It was a hypothetical question as there was no visa, but I needed to be honest with her.

I phoned Carla on Easter Sunday as I stood outside the lighthouse in the sunshine whilst seagulls watched and screeched. Discussing the fate of a homeless Ukrainian teenager whilst looking at glorious views of the sea and Dorset coastline seemed surreal. But I was glad I'd phoned as Carla made me feel better about the situation – she had grown fond of Yurii and said he was a pleasure to host. She would keep him as long as necessary and we'd work something out.

It was after we'd returned from Swanage that I had a lightbulb moment. If Yurii wasn't going to be allowed in as an unaccompanied teenager, then we needed to get him accompanied! For visa purposes I was sure this would need to be someone related to him, otherwise I could have linked his application to someone else whom I was helping. The obvious person was his mother.

I messaged Yurii with my idea and explained that she wouldn't need to stay with him, just travel with him. His response was muted; he said that he didn't think his mother would be able to get time off work. That didn't ring true with me as she could come to the UK then return to Poland immediately, over a weekend if necessary. And what kind of heartless employer would stop a mother from having a few days off to help her son to safety? Maybe he was worried that she would travel with him then decide to stay? He was very independent and seemed to be enjoying aspects of his new life; having his mother with him would have changed things. Anyway, I told him that it made sense for his mother to apply for a visa and to give all my details as the sponsor. He helped his mother do this on April 25th.

The next day I was contacted again by Radio Hereford and Worcester but this time the host was Elliot Webb. On air I gave an update on Yurii's visa situation and explained the rule change for unaccompanied teenagers. I deliberately did not mention that he was in France in case that was an excuse for turning down his application or putting it to the bottom of the pile. We had both jumped through all the hoops of the Homes for Ukraine scheme and we had submitted all the documents that had been requested. I'd had my home inspected and approved and a new enhanced DBS certificate issued. The local council knew who I was and where I was and that I was ready to give a home to a teenager from a war zone. Yet the official view seemed to be that it would be better for Yurii not to come to the UK.

BBC TV picked up my radio interview and asked if I would appear on Midlands Today the next day. This should have been straightforward but was preceded by a minor drama. I had returned from a dog walk in good time to get tidied up for my TV appearance, but as I walked into my house I could see water gushing through the ceiling into the kitchen. By the time I had found out what to do and stopped the leak, the interview call was fast approaching. Unfortunately our internet at home was being unreliable so I had planned to take the call at work to be sure of a good connection. But after sorting out the leak there was no time left to get changed so I jumped in the car and headed for Worcester. The rush hour and the crawling traffic meant it took me longer than normal to get in. I parked the car minutes before the interview was scheduled.

Sitting in my office in front of my computer, I tried to compose myself. My breathing was starting to return to normal but my face was still red and I was still wearing my dog walking clothes. I looked like I had just cleaned up a kitchen flood when Audrey Diaz started to interview me. Watching myself on the evening news later, I cringed that I hadn't had time to smarten myself up for my TV debut. A friend later commented that he'd seen my interview but it was a shame something was wrong with the colour as my face was red. Er yes, shame about the technical problem.

On April 27th, two days after his mother's visa application was submitted, I received a short message from Yurii:

'I have 2 visas now. OMG. For me and my mum at the same time.'

I felt a cold anticipatory shiver as I asked him to forward the visas to me so I could see if his was linked to his mother's in any way. I read them both carefully and there was nothing to say that he had to travel with his mother. We had beaten the system, although maybe I shouldn't be shouting about that. He was free to travel to the UK as soon as he wanted.

Chapter 15
London to Worcester –
April 2022

My head was thumping as I opened my eyes. I was prone to headaches but could normally identify what had caused them. On the 28th April I woke up with a bad head for no apparent reason, but at least I had nothing to get up for. Unusually it was about 9 am before I looked at my phone. There was a short Whatsapp message from Yurii:

'My train ticket says that I will arrive at 10.30.'

I was momentarily confused – was he arriving today? Did he mean evening or morning? Did he mean London or Worcester? By the time we'd exchanged a few messages, it was clear that he was already hurtling through Kent on the Eurostar and would be arriving in London in little over an hour's time. I had known he was going to travel as soon as possible, but thought I'd have enough notice to get to London to meet him myself or arrange for someone to meet him and accompany him to Paddington. But once again I hadn't counted on an impatient teenager.

Whilst I was working out a plan for meeting Yurii, he was comfortably seated on the train and plugged in to his final online lesson for his Ukrainian school syllabus. Finishing his lesson soon after the train emerged from the Channel Tunnel, he looked out the window as the gently rolling fields and orchards of Kent flashed by. His phone pinged and a message from my daughter Toni appeared.

Fortunately Toni worked in central London and was able to respond immediately to my plea for help and get herself to St Pancras in time to meet the Eurostar. She messaged Yurii to say that she would be waiting by the Welcome to Ukrainians stand and sent a photo of herself so he would recognise her; this stand was manned by volunteers and was draped in the bright blue and yellow of Ukraine. Within minutes of the train pulling in to the station he approached her with a big smile on his face, an overstuffed carrier bag in one hand, a rucksack on his back and a Ukrainian flag pinned to his lumberjack shirt. They said each other's names in confirmation as they opened their arms and hugged.

Toni had worked for Kingsway Summer School for three summers when she was a student so she was used to meeting and greeting foreign students and making them feel at ease. Obviously Yurii's situation was very different – he wasn't exactly in the UK for a short language learning holiday and the normal small talk questions about his journey, home and family might be inappropriate. However, as she guided him across London to Paddington, she was surprised at how similar he was to so many summer school teenagers. He asked questions about everything he was seeing for the first time and even wondered if there would be time to do a short tour of the city before catching the train to Worcester! Despite having grown up in a capital city himself and having gained worldliness in his travels, he seemed surprised at the size of London. Even the number of stations and underground lines made his eyes widen and his jaw drop.

A train to Worcester had just left and there was an hour to wait for the next one. Time passed quickly as they had some refreshments whilst Yurii told Toni stories about his journey. Some of the stories made her laugh, especially one where he described helping his Swiss host, Mathieu, write a letter to a Moldovan girl who had broken his heart – a 16-year-old helping a man twice his age! Toni was impressed by Yurii's confidence, his level of English and how relaxed he seemed. Many summer school teenagers were a bit self-conscious on arrival and often spoke minimally as they adjusted to being in an English-speaking environment. Yet this young boy, a refugee from war, was chatting to her like London was the latest stop on an Interrail holiday.

The departures board updated to indicate that the Worcester train would be leaving from platform 1. It was a barrier free platform so Toni walked with him to the carriage, passing the bronze statue of Paddington Bear on the way. The story of the immigrant bear arriving in London and relying on the kindness of strangers had obvious echoes with Yurii's situation and became symbolic for many Ukrainians passing through the station on their way to a new life. 'Remember there are three stations in Worcester. You need Foregate Street.' Toni said emphasising the last two words. He nodded in response and said 'OK' but she wasn't convinced he'd grasped the importance of what she was saying so repeated it and later texted him the name to make sure. He wouldn't be the first visitor to Worcester to get out at the wrong station. They said goodbye and Yurii settled in to yet another seat on yet another train

– hopefully the last for a while. He plugged in his phone then looked out the window at the vast iron and glass dome of Brunel's station as the Great Western train left Paddington on time.

Listening to the announcements at Slough and Reading, the teenager wondered whether his English was as good as he had thought. Was that really how you pronounced those towns? And the train's destination of Hereford – surely that's not how you said it? His English had served him well throughout his travels but now he was in the home of the language, he wondered if it was going to be good enough. Oxford didn't bring any pronunciation surprises with the station announcements but the station itself did. How could such a world famous city have such an unimpressive station? He peered out to see what the Oxford skyline had to offer, but there was nothing that matched the pictures in his school English text books. His thoughts were interrupted by the ticket inspector who came through the carriage asking to see tickets. He showed his passport and watched the look of surprise on the inspector's face. Ukrainian nationals were entitled to free train travel but the inspector's reaction suggested that this was the first time she'd been shown one. Her eyes expressed kindness and compassion as she wished him luck.

After Oxford the train passed through the Cotswolds with their pretty villages and names: Kingham, Moreton-in-Marsh, Honeybourne then on through Evesham and Pershore. The Malvern Hills could be spotted from the window as the train pulled in to the first of the three Worcester stations: Worcestershire Parkway, a name to make non-native speakers gulp and try to avoid saying. Yurii sat up straight on high alert and unplugged his phone. After Worcester Shrub Hill he had his first view of the city as the track curved round towards Foregate Street. He took in the industrial outskirts and builders' yards, glimpsed some boats in a marina and noted numerous church spires with the square tower of the cathedral dominating the view. The city seemed to be circled by trees and hills and everything was at a low level. Amazingly it seemed that no buildings were higher than the church spires and towers.

This was the point when Yurii and I were finally about to meet. I was on the platform as the dark green and yellow nose cone of the London train eased in to the station. It was almost exactly two months since the Russians had invaded Ukraine. Two months since Yurii's world had been turned upside down and he'd left his homeland, his family and his friends. Since then he'd travelled about 3,000 km through six different countries and been helped along his way by so many people, each one making his journey that little bit easier. And now he was almost at his journey's end.

He was easy to identify so I waved as he walked down the platform towards me. We hugged as I welcomed him to Worcester. Six weeks after we had first spoken to each other whilst he was in Switzerland, we finally got to meet. Like Toni, I was struck by how friendly, confident and relaxed he was and how well he spoke English. After such a

LEAVING UKRAINE

gruelling journey in such difficult circumstances he could have been traumatised, withdrawn or simply tired but he seemed ready to embrace his new life. In fact one of the first things he said as he got into my car was. *'Wow! How can you drive on the left?!'*

PART TWO

April 2022 – September 2024

Chapter 16
Settling In

As I came into the kitchen, Yurii was sitting on the sofa with a bowl of ice-cream.

'What are you eating?' I asked, although I was pretty sure I knew.

'Ice-cream,' he replied with a big smile on his face.

'Um ….. it's breakfast time,' I continued with furrowed brows, keeping my tone neutral. I was very aware of cultural differences, but knew that this situation wasn't one of those. I had created this situation by telling him yesterday that he could help himself to any food and drink in the house except alcohol.

'Do you have ice-cream for breakfast in Ukraine?' I asked with a look telling him that I wasn't born yesterday.

'No! But you told me I could have what I want,' he replied, reasonably enough.

I admitted that indeed I had, but then explained that ice-cream was not a breakfast food but an occasional treat. I'm sure he knew that but was testing what he could get away with. This was the first of a number of minor clashes over food in general and meals in particular. Each time he did something I found surprising, I asked what was normal in his culture and then explained what was normal in our household and that he was now part of our family so should try and adapt.

Whilst having the conversation about ice-cream, I was aware that we were due to leave home in about quarter of an hour as we had an appointment to visit the Royal Grammar School.

'You remember that you have an appointment at school very soon?' I reminded him, pointing at my watch and noting that he looked like he'd just got out of bed. Which he had.

'Yes. I am going to have a shower now,' he replied getting to his feet and stretching as if this was just an ordinary day and we were going to go for a stroll. In the space of a few minutes, I had become aware of two potential flashpoints around living with Yurii: the first was food and the second was timing. In these early days I would need to guide him gently towards doing things our way to fit in with our household and become one of the family.

'I don't want to be late for meeting the headmaster so you'd better hurry up,' I told him, aiming to sound brisk rather than irritated. 'When I say we are leaving at a certain time, I mean it,' I called after him as he disappeared upstairs. Later I introduced him to the family mantra of 'ROTD' which stands for 'Rolling off the Drive'. This was one of Rick's sayings to make sure that our kids understood that a departure time meant exactly that. It didn't mean the time to start looking for your shoes or your phone or having something to eat. It meant the time that he/we would be driving away.

That morning, against the odds, we did ROTD in time for our appointment at RGS. Yurii seemed remarkably calm about this visit which was going to include a tour of the school and an interview with the headmaster. As we drove into Worcester, I tried to put myself in his shoes – he had just arrived in a foreign country which was to be his home for the foreseeable future. He had to interact in a foreign language at all times, adapt to living with strangers, accept that Rick and I were *in loco parentis* and enter a completely different school system. And in the background his country was under attack and he was separated from his family and friends. Most people in his situation would have been at least a little bit stressed but Yurii behaved more like an exchange student than a refugee from war. Gazing out the car window he repeated his observation from the day before, '*Wow, I still can't believe you drive on the left!*'

I parked in front of Britannia House, one of the many elegant and historic buildings that make up RGS. This place was so familiar to me; I had been to countless parents' evenings and events during the fifteen years that my three children were pupils here and then I'd been Director of Kingsway Summer School which had been based at RGS for seven summers between 2013 and 2019. But today I was in a rather different role, a grey area somewhere between a step-parent and a guardian.

We were met in reception by Tom, an ex-pupil who was working as an intern in the school's marketing department. His job was to show us around and answer any questions prior to our meeting with the headmaster. Yurii took everything in his stride, asked intelligent questions and spoke politely to anyone who was introduced to him. He was particularly impressed with and excited by the Chemistry Department. This was one of his favourite subjects and his eyes lit up at the facilities and possibilities.

Beneath his cool exterior, he must have felt like he'd stumbled on to the set of Hogwarts. You feel a sense of history and privilege in the school's beautiful old buildings, the wood panelled halls, the vaulted roofs and stained glass windows. The portraits of severe looking head teachers are intimidating and the memorials to staff and pupils who died in the world wars are sobering. Even though I was very familiar with the school's facilities, I couldn't help trying to see them through Yurii's eyes. His Ukrainian school had a number, School 194 Perspective, rather than a name and had its roots in Soviet Russia whereas the RGS buildings could be the setting for Tom Brown's School Days.

The clock was chiming 12.00 as we crossed the manicured lawns of the quad for our appointment with Mr John Pitt, the headmaster. He was joined by the Head of Sixth Form and the two of them gave Yurii a friendly welcome and asked him questions about his school subjects in Ukraine and what he'd like to continue studying. I felt a maternal pride in Yurii's performance as if I had brought up this polite, articulate and intelligent young man myself. Both men were complimentary about his level of English and his maturity and felt that RGS would be the right place for him if he could satisfy the tutors that his subject knowledge was high enough to embark on A level studies in Maths, Chemistry and Computer Science.

The talk then moved on to other ways in which the school could support Yurii. Mr Pitt was sure that the school's catering service would provide lunches free of charge and he also felt that the school's transport service would like to play their part and provide lifts from Ombersley to school and back without charge. These things he would check but, in the meantime, he said Yurii would need to wear a smart business suit and tie to school. He offered to see if there could be financial help for the suit which I declined as I felt the school was doing enough, but I accepted the offer of a school tie. We left RGS feeling impressed with the school's generosity and readiness to give practical help in this unusual situation.

The following week Yurii met his subject tutors and was assessed as being a suitable candidate to embark on A level studies. He was officially offered a place at RGS along with free school lunches and transport and told that his situation would be reviewed at Christmas. Everything had come together perfectly except the timing. This wasn't ideal as he would be joining the lower sixth in the final half-term of the academic year, but he was keen to get back to his school work after three months of dislocation. He would be thrown in the deep end with an established year group but one thing Yurii didn't lack was confidence.

Part of the Homes for Ukraine scheme involved a £200 welcome payment to help new arrivals buy essentials and get settled in. As Yurii had all his essentials taken care of, I suggested that he might like to spend the money on buying a suit for school. He was happy to do this, so we went along to M&S where he tried on his first ever suit and we ordered one that was the right size for his extra tall and extra skinny frame along with some shirts.

It was the eve of his first day at school that we discovered he had never worn a tie and didn't have a clue what to do with it. Watching someone teach someone how to tie a tie is quite entertaining so, whilst Rick did his best, I made myself less useful by videoing the two of them and laughing. Yurii liked to excel in anything he tried so, within half an hour, he was a master of the art of knotting a tie. Once dressed in a suit and tie and wearing the smart shoes that his mum had sent him he was utterly transformed from a scruffy, travelling teenager into a smart and polished young man. He looked ready for the challenge of joining the lower sixth at RGS.

Chapter 17
Leisure Time

He smiled with delight as he read through the document I had handed him, 'It's the first time I've had a personal assistant!' he said jumping up and down as if on a pogo stick. There were times when I did feel like his PA, and organising a rota of lifts to get him to and from basketball practice was one of those admin tasks that I did regularly over the next few years.

Soon after he arrived, I had emailed the Worcester Wolves Under 17 basketball club and explained Yurii's situation including the fact that he had been in a basketball team in Kyiv. They were kind enough to give him a free place in the club, but this required a commitment to two or three evening practices a week at different times in different venues which meant he'd need four or six return lifts per week excluding matches. One of the venues was in Worcester, but the other was in Martley. This village is only about eight miles from Ombersley, but it's along winding, unlit country lanes – it wouldn't be a particularly nice drive during the winter months. Making sure he was in the right place at the right time was going to require accurate information from the club which I needed to pass on to the SUN volunteers.

The SUN group was set up to help refugees in the village, so I asked them for volunteer drivers to get Yurii to and from his basketball practices. The response was good, sufficient for me to share out the lifts amongst about eight people. There were drivers who preferred to do the outbound lifts in the early evening and those who preferred the homebound ones at 10 pm. I created a rota which showed who was doing which lift on which date to which venue. I also had to make it crystal clear where Yurii was to meet the driver and what car to look out for, especially in the early days before he'd met all his taxi drivers. So much could go wrong but it rarely did. It normally took me a few hours to put a rota together and it would last for a term until new dates and venues and driver availability had to be entered into a new rota.

As our house is slightly tricky to find, I decided that Yurii would meet the drivers at the bus-stop opposite the medical centre, which is only about 200 metres away from our house. All locals would know this place and there was a lay-by where cars could stop safely. He would need four minutes to walk to the bus-stop so if he allowed ten minutes he would be there in good time and wouldn't keep anyone waiting. As the meeting time approached, I would call out time checks to try and get him moving, but it took a while and a few spats for me to change his cavalier attitude to time:

'Yurii, it's 7.15 pm – you'll need to leave in 5 minutes.' I'd shout up the stairs.

'OK.' came the reply.

'Yurii, it's 7.20 pm – you need to leave NOW!'

'Yes – don't worry.'

'Yurii, it's 7.25 pm – you're going to be late.'

Then he'd appear at or after the time he was due to meet his lift. I'd wait until he was home before I'd give him the lecture on how disrespectful it is to keep people waiting, especially when they are doing you a favour. They could be late picking him up but he shouldn't ever be late for them. He did eventually improve his time-keeping, but it took being late for public transport to help him change his ways. With the 303 bus being an hourly service, he would only inconvenience himself if he was late for it.

There was one incident at the bus-stop which we found amusing but the other person involved certainly wasn't laughing. On this particular occasion he was at the bus-stop before his lift, when a car pulled up. He walked up to the passenger door, opened it and started to get in. The female driver shrieked at him to get out then drove off at speed. We think she was probably there to meet someone from the bus. Did that incident teach him to pay more attention to the information I gave him about the driver's car? Hmm maybe.

In addition to his basketball sessions, he was also invited to join Ombersley Tennis Club at no charge. As he could walk or cycle to the club, I decided to keep myself out of any arrangements. If he was late, he could deal with it. If he'd forgotten what time he was due there, he could deal with that too. He had never played tennis before coming to the UK but, by all accounts, (especially his own, 'I think I was excellent!') he made rapid progress and became quite a decent player. He was a very competitive person so doing well and winning were really important to him. I used to try and teach him that winning wasn't everything but, as I didn't get through to him with that idea, I changed tack and used to call out to him, 'Don't bother coming home if you don't win!' Fortunately he understood my sarcasm and has a sense of humour and always called back 'OK I won't!' I never knew if he meant he wouldn't come home or he wouldn't lose but he always came home.

Being Yurii's PA meant being present for the regular visits from Children's Services. These were every six weeks even after they established during their first visit that their client was a mature, capable, independent teenager with no issues regarding his new living situation. During the first meeting, I had to exercise great self-control during this exchange:

Social worker: 'So how long do you think Yurii will be with you?'

Me: 'That will depend on Mr Putin.'

Social worker: 'Is he one of Yurii's teachers?'

Me: 'No he's the President of Russia.'

Social worker: 'Oh right.'

Also during the first meeting, there was this exchange, barely out of my hearing:

Social worker (in a stage whisper): 'Are you happy here?'

Yurii: 'Yes. If I wasn't, I would leave.'

And he absolutely would.

To amuse ourselves before a visit, Yurii and I would come up with outlandish scenarios:

Me: 'When they ask what you do in your spare time, tell them you help with the cannabis crop upstairs.'

Yurii: 'Yes I'll make sure I'm wearing old clothes and tell them I don't get fed often.'

Me: 'And tell them you're a modern slave. We don't do old-fashioned slavery here.'

Yurii: 'Of course. I'll tell them that I've learned lots about drug distribution.'

Me: 'Yes. And tell them we never make you work later than midnight, except at weekends.'

Of course the social worker would come and we would both behave ourselves, but occasionally Yurii would catch my eye or vice versa and we'd smile at the conversation that was just beneath the surface.

The social workers were doing their job and ticking their boxes, but I felt that home visits every six weeks for a teenager who clearly wasn't vulnerable was a poor use of their time. I suggested that they should leave it longer between visits and maybe have a phone call or video call with him in between seeing him at home. Or even check with the school safeguarding team. On one occasion I got the reply that seeing Yurii was a nice visit to do, but that was hardly a good use of their resources. One of my issues with the frequency of the visits was that their time could be better spent with a vulnerable child who actually needed their help. We know that social workers are overstretched and have too many cases to look after, so someone needed to look at Yurii's situation and do something different. But they didn't and the visits continued until he was 18.

Chapter 18
Charming the Locals

'Well that's really pathetic!' I said to him, shaking my head in mock disappointment. 'You're going to have to do better than that if you want to live with us.' The two of us were standing in the field next to the house. Yurii had just tried to throw a ball using the launcher whilst the dogs were dancing around excitedly waiting to see where the ball would go. It didn't go anywhere. I took the launcher from him and, with a smug smile on my face, sent one ball on a long, high arc to the far end of the field then sent a second ball in the opposite direction. Both dogs raced away to retrieve the balls. I enjoyed the feeling that I could do something physical which this young, fit, athletic boy couldn't, but my superiority at this skill only lasted about two minutes.

To fit into our household, it was essential that Yurii bonded with Barney and Bella. Not only did he bond with them immediately, but he also understood their personalities and played along with our surreal, in-family fantasy dialogues. These dialogues involved giving Barney the voice of a neurotic New Yorker, such as Woody Allen, with the catchphrase 'I get anxious.' We gave him this voice because he was a very anxious dog. Obviously. His anxiety could be triggered by a long list of people from the milkman to anyone delivering anything. And squirrels. And other mammals. Pigeons too. He was also a bit of a dope but would get riled when we questioned his intelligence and we'd say on his behalf, 'Don't call me stoopid!' in the voice used by Kevin Kline in A Fish Called Wanda. Yurii joined in but never quite mastered the American accent despite having an extraordinary command of English.

Bella had a completely different personality as she was super smart and highly academic. She too had the voice of an American, but hers was a whiney west coast accent. Not sure why she had an American accent, maybe because she was Barney's sister. Anyway Bella's ongoing story was that she was an intellectual and always writing a PhD thesis which she never finished. We'd have conversations with her where she'd explain her calculations in a nerdy way. Well Yurii understood that and joined in with the insane story line as if this was completely normal. Maybe it's just us.

Yurii got to know more Ombersley locals in his first few weeks with us than we had managed in over 30 years. There were the SUN taxi drivers who took him to & from basketball practice and there were people who gave him pocket money in return for doing odd jobs: for one neighbour he looked after her tortoises whenever she was away, for another he cut the grass. He did a variety of gardening jobs and he was given some one-off projects such as cleaning cars and even the very niche task of polishing the badges on vintage cars. From time to time he was paid to be a waiter at a party or event.

As he got to know people he was invited to different occasions and events where he met yet more locals. He was open to anything and accepted an invitation to a Young Farmers' BBQ and even to a church service. He must have got a very warped idea of the cars that normal people drive as he would often come home and jig with joy as he described the car he'd just had a lift in – the list included an Aston Martin, a Porsche a BMW convertible and a Jaguar. But obviously most lifts he got were in more modest cars, including mine.

Ombersley people were so generous; one person, whom he'd never met, regularly sent him cash for no reason. He was also given a bike, a play-station and clothes. I understood why. Every day we saw horrific scenes of what Putin's army were doing in Ukraine and here, in our midst, was a young Ukrainian who had escaped from that world. By helping Yurii, people must have felt they were helping Ukraine. In reality he had so much whilst many of those who couldn't leave Ukraine had so little.

It was against this backdrop of generosity that Yurii and I had a minor clash when he announced during his first summer that he was going to apply for Universal Credit. I looked at him in astonishment and reminded him that he was a 17-year-old with no dependants and all his expenses taken care of. From his teenage point of view it was free money and he had nothing to lose by applying for it. He must have been encouraged to do this by people he'd met in local support groups, people who knew more about benefits than their responsibilities to their host country. I explained to him that there is no such thing as free money, it was British taxpayers' money and that we taxpayers were already covering all his expenses. This was an early example of a black and white situation where I had to make our values clear. His application went no further.

In contrast to that particular situation, most Ukrainians I was involved with were keen to get a job, earn their own money and become independent of their hosts as soon as possible. Professional people who couldn't work in their field of expertise, due to language issues or their qualifications not being accepted here, worked in any job they could get and could get to given the transport problems. So I knew of lawyers, doctors and architects doing cleaning jobs or working in care homes or bars.

To be fair on Yurii, he understood that he had landed on his feet. One evening he insisted on coming to the SUN meeting but didn't tell me why. He arrived after me, deliberately I think, so that he could make an entrance. He liked the limelight. Looking very smart in his school suit, worn for impact, he sat down and listened as we went round the table giving updates on what we had been doing or what help we could offer or needed. When it came to Yurii's turn, he stood up, again for impact, and made an eloquent and heartfelt speech of thanks to everyone. He knew how to charm people and his speech did exactly that.

Whilst new arrivals from Ukraine settled into living and working in Ombersley, Yurii was turning into an independent RGS sixth former, catching the minibus from outside the dentist's every morning. Once he missed it and was cheeky enough to knock on the door of an elderly lady who lived nearby to ask if she could give him a lift to school. She was a member of the SUN group and he'd often say hello or wave to her on his way to and from the bus. To be fair she had told him to call if ever he needed anything; that's exactly what he did and got himself a lift to school.

He also managed to charm at least one of the minibus drivers by shaking hands with him every day as he got on and off the bus. He found out about the impression he'd made via the school librarian who was married to the driver. She approached him in the library one day and said, '*My husband thinks you're great!*' and explained how he was impressed by Yurii's daily interactions. Such behaviour is not very British, and who knows what the other school kids thought of this. I imagine there was some eye-rolling but fair play to Yurii for doing what felt right to him rather than what other people were doing or not doing.

Home life with our extra resident settled into an easy rhythm. I generally didn't see him on weekdays until about 5 pm when he got in from school. We'd have a brief chat about his day, often whilst he was grazing on leftovers from the fridge. Then he would disappear to his room and I wouldn't see him again until dinner time; we always ate together except on nights when he had basketball or tennis. If he was eating with us he would help with clearing up afterwards and then go to his room. He was like most teenagers in that he appeared at meal times and then was happy doing his own thing the rest of the time. Most of the time he was very easy to live with.

Chapter 19
Independent Thinking

I peered out of the study window, looking down the lane into the darkness. It had been nearly 10 years since I'd worried about the whereabouts of my own teenage children and here I was again with that old, familiar feeling: ice running through my blood and a dull stomach ache. I'd never been one to panic but I was very good at dreaming up worst case scenarios. Tonight I was imagining that Yurii had been in a road traffic accident, possibly along one of the nearby unlit lanes. He could be lying injured somewhere or maybe he'd already been taken to hospital and there was nothing to identify who he was or where he lived.

It was a warm May bank holiday weekend and that evening we'd had dinner in the garden. Our kids were home for a few days and we'd all been catching the last of the sun and chatting when Yurii announced that he was going for a bike ride. He'd only been gifted the bike the day before so I understood that he wanted to try it out. As he got up from the table, my final words to him were, 'Don't forget we drive on the left here!'

Before long the sun disappeared, the temperature started to drop and dusk crept in. We put away the garden cushions and moved indoors. That was when I realized that Yurii had been gone for some time. He hadn't said where he was going, but I had assumed that he would be cycling around the village, getting used to the bike and exploring the neighbourhood.

Had I been irresponsible in not giving him a time to be home or finding out where he intended to go? What would the police think of my careless parenting if I had to get them involved?

By 9.45 pm he'd been gone nearly two hours and it was dark. It was only then that it occurred to me that he might have taken his phone with him. I called his number expecting it to ring out but he picked up instantly.

'Yurii – where are you?'

'I'm in Worcester.'

'What?! Why? Where?'

'By the river, opposite the cathedral. Why?'

He had cycled nearly 10 miles from our house in the evening without a helmet on a bike with no lights. I was astonished and annoyed.

'Come home straight away and keep off the A449! We'll discuss this later.'

I now had plenty of time to imagine this boy, who had left a war zone to find safety, meeting his end on the notorious local A road. How would I tell his parents that he'd only survived a few weeks in peaceful, rural England? I stared out of the window trying to predict when he would appear. Thirty minutes passed …. then forty … then forty five. Should I get in the car and go and look for him? At 10.30 pm his pale face appeared out of the darkness. Relief mixed with disbelief as I tried to make it clear that what he did was dangerous and irresponsible. Like most teenagers he considered himself invincible, but he apologized at the same time as assuring me that,

'It was fine. I have good eyesight even without lights.'

'It's not about your eyesight. It's about other road-users being able to see you.'

'I trust myself.'

'That's not the point. We need to get you some lights and, in future, you should always let me know where you are going. If you had told me you intended to go to Worcester this evening, I would have stopped you! And you need to wear a helmet!'

Maybe he was used to more freedom in Kyiv. Maybe his mum would leave him to his own devices, including what time he went out and whether or not he rode his bike in the dark without lights or a helmet. I didn't know and I didn't ask as it was irrelevant. I was responsible for his safety whilst he was living with us and I had the same expectations of him as I'd had of my own children when they were his age.

Other flashpoints were less serious but reflected his fierce independence and some firmly held opinions. There were little things such as when I offered to explain the 303 bus service to him:

'I'll be fine.'

I could understand why he said he'd be fine, having made his way on his own all the way from Ukraine to Worcester, but he didn't know that the northbound 303 and the southbound 303 both come to the same bus stop in Ombersley. You have to look at the front of the bus to see if it is going to Kidderminster or Worcester. He got on the first one that came along and before long realized that he was heading away from Worcester. He got off as soon as he could and the driver directed him to cross the road to wait for the Worcester bound 303. This he did and 30 minutes later the same driver on the same bus picked him up! It made me laugh and made for a good story but illustrated how listening to advice would have saved him some time and trouble.

There were other discussions around public transport such as when he needed to get to Birmingham airport for an early morning flight and he told me he'd get a train:

'I doubt you'll get a train at that time in the morning.'

'I think there will be one.'

'Why do you think there will be one? Have you looked at the timetable?'

'No.'

'Well I bet you won't be able to get to the airport in time for check-in. You'll need a lift.'

Of course he needed a lift and of course he was trying to be independent and not cause any additional hassle for me. But I sometimes felt he would argue that black was white.

There were other occasions when I tried to get him to understand that I had his best interests at heart and that maybe I had some advice worth listening to. I had bought him some Crocs for his 17th birthday and he was absolutely delighted with them to the extent that he barely took them off. One day he asked if he could join me for a walk with the dogs:

'Of course but you'd better change into some walking shoes.'

'I'll be fine.'

'I'm planning on walking about 5 miles. Crocs aren't made for distances.'

'I'll be fine.'

Maybe he was fine, but he couldn't keep up a decent walking pace and I imagine his feet were shredded by the activity. For at least his first year with us he continued to wear Crocs or flip-flops for long, country walks even though he had trainers and more suitable shoes.

One hot and sunny day we were going off for a walk with the dogs when I suggested that he should put on some sun-cream,

'It's OK – I don't need it.'

'Have you heard about skin cancer and protecting your skin?'

'I don't think sun cream works. If it did, everyone would wear it and there would be no skin cancer.'

I always kept in mind that he was a young boy arguing in a foreign language, but sometimes I didn't know where to begin. We had a long walk so I had plenty of time to talk about scientific evidence as well as the cost of sun cream. I didn't know what effect my words had had until the following summer when, on a very hot day, he asked where the sun cream was as he didn't want to get skin cancer. He was off to the Malvern Hills and he made a point of telling me that he was wearing trainers not Crocs. I smiled and congratulated him on his good sense.

On some occasions my parenting style was in direct conflict with what he expected or was used to. He texted me from school one day:

'Can you get me a thermometer please?'

'Why do you need a thermometer?'

'I feel really ill.'

'A thermometer won't make you feel better.'

'I really need one.'

I have never used a thermometer with my children or myself and don't have one in the house. I'd have to buy one, google what to do with it and find out what the normal temperature range was. That wasn't my style and I didn't feel that Yurii feeling unwell warranted a change in my well-established approach to illness. However, I take illness seriously and have a well-stocked medical cupboard with medication to cover most situations. When Yurii got home, I listened to his symptoms, gave him some advice and offered him some meds. But all he wanted was a thermometer or a doctor's appointment.

'You'll be better before you could get a doctor's appointment. You probably have man flu. You need to have a warm bath, take some Lemsip and go to bed.'

His upbringing had taught him not to have a bath when you're ill and not to take painkillers without first taking your temperature. I shrugged and said we'd review his condition the next day.

The next day he appeared looking dreadful but not visibly feverish. He collapsed into a chair and closed his eyes so I could see just how bad things were. I was about to take the dogs for a walk so I gave him some advice before leaving,

'You look awful. Have a bath or shower. Wash your hair. Take some paracetomol.'

When I returned a couple of hours later, he was transformed. His hair was clean, his eyes were shining and he said in utter amazement,

'The pills worked and I had a bath!'

I was pleased that he had taken my advice on this occasion and that he'd seen the improvement in his condition. But as a joke I bought him a thermometer for his next birthday.

There was a more important flashpoint around scientific evidence that I had to handle very carefully. Yurii had been with us a few weeks when our local GP practice invited him to come in for a Covid jab. I urged him to take up the offer and was met with a wall of resistance. No way was he going to get vaccinated; he came up with the usual arguments against vaccination that I have no time for because I believe in science and experts. I was already aware that there was widespread vaccine hesitancy amongst Ukrainians, and I later read that Putin encouraged this, long before he attacked the country. The Russian president wanted all countries within his orbit to be suspicious of anything the West offered as help. A few Ukrainians that I'd found homes for could not proceed because they refused to get vaccinated. That astonished me – their fears of the vaccine were so deep-rooted that they'd rather stay in a war zone than oblige their potential hosts by getting vaccinated.

I had fully supported British hosts who'd said they wanted their potential guests to either be vaccinated already or be willing to get vaccinated in the UK. But I was in a different situation with Yurii. He was already living with us – getting vaccinated hadn't been a concern when I was trying to get him to the UK. Now he was here but refusing to get the jab. He'd studied chemistry at school so, of course, he was a teenaged expert. I knew that if I pushed him, he would leave and take his chances; he was sufficiently strong-minded and independent to do that. So I backed off from a major row and, instead, I sent him the link to the Dimbleby Lecture given by Professor Dame Sarah Gilbert explaining the science behind the Oxford vaccine and how it was produced so quickly. He didn't mention it again, but I hope he watched the video and reflected on the thoughtful, decades long, evidence based work done by some of the most distinguished scientists in the world.

Chapter 20
Give and Take

The dinner table was set for the three of us and I was standing at the hob stirring a bubbling pan of tomato sauce. Yurii came into the kitchen, took a small saucepan from the cupboard and some eggs from the fridge. 'What are you doing?' I asked, frowning at him. 'I'm going to have some boiled eggs,' he replied and, failing to read my body language or tone of voice, continued what he was doing.

'Can you see that I'm cooking dinner? We'll be eating within half an hour,' I said trying to keep my voice neutral.

'Yes it's OK. My grandmother says that if I eat before a meal then I still have to eat the meal. I will do that,' he replied as if that settled the matter. Although I understood where his grandmother was coming from, that was not going to work in my house and he needed to know why:

'Well I wouldn't let my own children do what you're doing and I'm treating you the same as I did them. You're one of our family now. It takes time and effort to cook a meal and I'd like you to feel ready to eat, not half full. Dinner will be on the table very soon,' I said firmly.

To be fair on Yurii, if you gave him a clear rationale for doing or not doing something he generally accepted it, although there was often a bit of an argument first. He returned the eggs to the fridge and the three of us had dinner together.

He hadn't been used to eating en famille, but it was something he enjoyed; he told me that he loved the evening meal the four of them had together at Carla's house in Paris. This was routine in our family home too so we ate together as often as his busy schedule allowed. I always cooked enough for a passing coach party to drop in unexpectedly for a meal, so normally there were leftovers which Yurii liked to have the next day when he got in from school. He was methodical about eating leftover food in date order, and was as committed as I was to not wasting food.

Yurii was an easy person to cook for as he enjoyed his food and was open to trying new things. He'd sometimes sit on a stool in the kitchen, watching me whilst I was cooking, and ask questions about what I was doing. His favourite dishes included shepherd's pie, Thai chicken soup, spaghetti carbonara and burger and chips. Despite being a big meat eater he got used to the fact that I cook a lot of vegetarian food; I would test him (and Rick) whilst we were eating and ask them to tell me if the meal had meat in it or not. My not so subtle point was that meat wasn't essential to a nice meal. He also loved desserts and was particularly taken with one called lemon crunch pie which I'd never made before he came to stay so it became 'Yurii's dessert'.

Some of his eating habits were most probably cultural, although unusual to us, so I'd discuss what he was doing before leaving him to get on with it. He liked to add gherkins, spring onions, capers or hot chilli sauce to practically any meal – even a roast dinner. We'd sometimes have jokey tussles when I'd ask him if he'd like to taste the food before adding tabasco or some other unlikely ingredient to it. Realising that he'd had to get used to a completely different diet living with us, I made borscht every so often to try and give him a taste of home. This Ukrainian soup is delicious and far more than the sum of its parts and Yurii was very polite and appreciative of my efforts. However, working with the key ingredient of beetroot left my hands looking like they were dripping with blood and my kitchen was the crime scene.

We included Yurii whenever we had people round for lunch or dinner. He enjoyed acting as one of the hosts, keeping everyone topped up with drinks, but he was confident and mature enough to initiate conversations and ask people about themselves too. Although he loved being the centre of attention, he also made sure that he wasn't just answering questions. Yurii's transition to living with us went incredibly smoothly, but there was an incident at the beginning of his stay which caused Rick some concern. 'I don't know whether to knock on the bathroom door to see if Yurii is OK. I think he might have collapsed in the shower' he said trying not to sound alarmed.

'Why do you think that?'

'The water has been running for at least 15 minutes.'

'Hmm – let's leave it for a bit.'

The water stopped after 20 minutes or so and I later explained to Yurii about keeping showers short to save water, energy and costs. I can be in and out of a shower in about three minutes, including washing my hair, so I told him to aim for that kind of time but five minutes was OK. His first response was that he would shower less often in order to have longer showers. This was typical Yurii so I had to insist on doing things our way in our house. He did.

Despite our jokes about Yurii being a modern slave, he had very little to do around the house. Apart from helping clear up after dinner, he was responsible for emptying the kitchen compost bin and looking after the dogs from time to time. He also had to do his own ironing. I don't think he'd ever used an iron before coming to us so Rick gave him a masterclass in ironing as his standards and skills are significantly higher than mine. Once competent in ironing he chose to iron only his school shirts and to go for the casual, crumpled look with everything else.

A special task I gave him was to set up my trail camera at different places in our garden, regularly review the pictures and let me know if there was anything interesting to see. I'd had the camera for a couple of years but hadn't got into the habit of using it. Whilst he was setting the camera up for the first time, he saw two animals that he couldn't identify so came running into the house calling excitedly for me to come and see. At the bottom of our field were two muntjak deer. I knew there were a number in our area but I had never seen them in our garden before. Thanks to Yurii taking responsibility for my camera, I found all kinds of wildlife visited us when I wasn't looking.

Although having little to do regularly in the way of household chores, he was very helpful with other things. He would often help Rick with furniture moving at Kingsway House. There were so many weekends when Rick needed to move chairs and desks from one room to another so having a young, fit and willing helper was useful. We'd joke that he could set himself up in business as *'Yurii's Removals – No Job too Small, Most Jobs too Big.'*

He also helped by running the bar for us at our Kingsway House charity networking events. These were events that we hosted twice a year: in the summer and at Christmas. So according to the season he would be serving Pimm's or mulled wine to our clients. He enjoyed being a barman as it put him at the centre of the action and he could chat with people whilst serving them. These skills were also useful at the charity quizzes that Rick and I had hosted regularly in Ombersley village hall for nearly 25 years. We'd started doing this in the year 2000 to raise money for a hall for Sytchampton School, the local primary school which our children attended. The hall was eventually built long after our children had moved on but we did our bit when we could and others did theirs in their time.

The quizzes made decent money but they were also popular and good fun so we continued after our children had left Sytchampton. Over the following decades we raised money for various local clubs & charities, food banks, the church roof and in 2022 for Ukraine. Even though the first of our Ukraine quizzes was only ten days after he'd arrived, Yurii seemed totally relaxed being on a team with locals and helping with setting up and clearing up afterwards. He even asked me for the microphone at the end of his first quiz to announce that he'd found a pair of glasses. That was astonishingly confident – most native speakers would have asked me to make an announcement rather than speak to a hall full of more than 100 people.

In a short space of time Yurii had adapted to the way Rick and I lived, settled into school, committed to basketball and tennis clubs, undertaken some jobs to earn pocket money and formed friendly relationships with a significant number of Ombersley residents. He seemed to me like a boy on a school exchange trip – lapping up experiences, making the most of opportunities and enjoying life.

Chapter 21
Parental Distance

I scrolled through the online pictures of flowers until I found an arrangement of roses, snapdragons and chrysanthemums which I liked, priced at a suitable mid-way point between extravagance and budget. It was a blend of cool colours that I was always drawn to: pinks, blues and mauves mixed with white. I clicked on the link, added it to basket and arranged for it to be delivered to Carla's home in Paris. She'd done a fantastic job of looking after Yurii for five weeks whilst he was waiting for his visa, so it was a small gesture of thanks from me.

On receiving the flowers, she messaged me:

'The flowers are lovely – thank you! Funny that you're sending me a gift for looking after someone else's child when I didn't even get a message from his own parents.'

'Nothing at all? Really? Was he in contact with them?'

'Yes he spoke to them regularly and he phoned his grandmother one day to get a recipe.'

'They didn't send a message to you via Yurii?'

'No nothing.'

That was strange as Yurii was such a polite and considerate young man. He'd obviously been brought up by people who knew what constituted good manners. He understood the importance of saying thank you to British people, even for small things like being given a lift to a place the driver was going anyway. It had always surprised me that so many of our summer school students would just get out of the car, slam the door, say goodbye and walk away. He didn't.

He thanked me after every meal; after I'd done his washing; after I'd changed his bed; after I'd been to a school event with him: after I'd bought something he liked from the supermarket or allowed him to use my computer. He thanked me far more than I expected to be thanked, which I assumed was a part of his upbringing.

He also knew how to give compliments and would notice things like perfume or a new haircut and say something nice. Although I was on the receiving end of his compliments from time to time, I'd also hear him say complimentary things to others such as 'Nice dress!' or 'I like your shirt.' It was part of his charm and politeness which either he'd been taught or he'd copied from someone in his life.

His parents were alive and well and in regular contact with him. His mother was with his sister and grandmother in Poland; his father had to stay in Ukraine and be available for military service if required. I tried to imagine what it was like having your teenage son living thousands of miles away with another family. In this situation I'm sure I would feel relief that he was safely away from the horrors of war and gratitude that strangers had welcomed my son into their homes and lives. I'm sure I'd message to introduce myself and thank them, using Google translate if I didn't speak their language. I'd be hungry for news about his new life to compare with whatever he was telling me himself. But maybe there was some complicating factor that I wasn't aware of.

I received confirmation that his parents were happy with Yurii's situation via a social work assessment carried out by Worcestershire County Council. In the report it was stated that, *'neither parent raised any safeguarding concerns. They both speak highly of Sue and Rick. His dad said they take care of him as if he were their own son and his mum said I know he is safe and he really enjoys living with Sue and Rick.'*

It was nice to read such comments but would have meant more to have heard from the parents directly. I didn't want anything from them, but I would have liked them to have checked that this was the case.

The days, weeks and months ticked by and I heard nothing from them. I didn't want Yurii to feel responsible for their lack of contact so I didn't make any pointed comments, but from time to time I asked if they were OK, especially after attacks on Kyiv where his father was still living. At the end of August 2022 Yurii went to Poland to meet up with his mother, grandmother and sister. When he returned he unpacked his bag in front of me, gave the dogs some Polish treats and showed me the new clothes that he'd been bought. I felt sure that he was going to produce a letter for me from his family but there was nothing.

Eventually I decided to pretend that Social Services were surprised that his parents hadn't been in contact with me. His response was pure Yurii,

'If you want them to call you, I'll ask them.'

'That's not the point. I'm surprised that they don't want to talk to me, to find out something about the people you are living with.'

'I've told them. They trust me.'

'What do you mean?'

'They know that if I was unhappy I would tell them and I would leave.'

He either didn't find it strange or couldn't think how else to respond to my comments. I found the situation baffling but, as a result of this conversation, Yurii set up a call with me and his father, Sasha. He was charming and grateful and his English was good enough for us to have a meaningful conversation. We had a few more conversations over the years and each time he expressed his gratitude for how Rick and I were helping Yurii.

His mother's English was, apparently, not very good so there was no phone call from her. Yurii had been with us for 15 months before I received an email from her apologising for taking so long to write but thanking me for looking after her son. She also apologised for her English. I replied the same day telling her to write in Ukrainian as I lived with someone who could translate for me. I didn't hear any more from her.

Chapter 22
Holidays

Sunny images of our family on holiday tumbled through my mind: our grown-up children, their partners and the dogs against the backdrop of boats, beaches and glorious scenery. I loved those weeks when we'd all get together and stay in a cottage by the sea. The days were normally spent on long walks punctuated by café or pub stops and the evenings hinged around having a nice meal and a few drinks. We never went away during the school holidays as we didn't need to - why would we choose to pay top rates to go at the most crowded time? That's what was bothering me: school holidays. After ten years of not having to think about school terms, I had put myself back in that situation.

We had booked a large house on the cliff top overlooking one of my favourite beaches, Rhossili, on the Gower Peninsular in Wales. This is an amazing expanse of empty golden sands and even on a sunny day there are only ever a handful of people there; the steep climb down to the beach and total lack of facilities mean you need to be committed to walking, surfing or swimming. I had decided that that was where I wanted to spend my birthday so had booked a year in advance to be sure of being exactly where I wanted to be, when I wanted to be there and with all the family able to join us.

Given the situation in Ukraine, it seemed shallow and self-indulgent to be fretting about holidays, but cancelling our plans wouldn't have helped the war effort. At the same time, I couldn't pull Yurii out of school and I couldn't leave him home alone before he was 18 or Social Services would have been sending their scarce resources to deal with me. There had to be a solution and there was.

The solution came via the holiday relief suggested by the SUN group during the inaugural meeting. There were three couples who didn't host anyone permanently but supported those of us who were; they were crucial to ensuring that Rick and I could make plans without worrying about school terms. Over the following years I would let them know when we were going to be away and we'd work out a cover plan for Yurii.

Max and Diane were well-known in Ombersley, having run the local bakery for twenty-seven years before they retired in 2017. Their home, Radnor House, in the centre of the village opposite the memorial hall and playing field, no longer had the little café tables outside nor the notice boards advertising hot pork rolls and coffee. The shop itself, once full of freshly baked bread, pies and quiches had been absorbed back into their home and the charcoal black canopy, printed with the name Ombersley Bakery, had gone. Since we'd moved to the village in 1988, the bakery had joined a long list of small businesses that had disappeared including a hardware store, a garden shed where we could buy fruit and vegetables, the post office, the newsagents, the previous bakery, a hairdresser's, a little art gallery and Everton's, a grocer's which could rival the food hall at Harrods for its range of unusual foods and ingredients. Fortunately new businesses had sprung up in different places and the three pubs had kept going so there was still plenty of life in the village.

Max and Di would welcome Yurii into their home and life on some of the occasions that Rick and I were away. Their proximity to the school bus stop meant that he could get from his bed to the bus in seconds when necessary. And sometimes it was. After school and at weekends they would invite him to join them and their grandchildren for walks, cycle rides or a trip to the Droitwich lido or he'd go to the allotment with Di to pick fruit or vegetables for dinner. One midsummer's evening they walked along the footpaths edging the barley and rhubarb fields and up to the ridge by Millhampton Wood; there they looked across the valley to Abberley and watched the sky turn glorious shades of pink and orange at sunset.

For Yurii's 18th birthday Max took him to Ombersley golf club and taught him to swing a club on the driving range and practise putting on the green. It was the teenager's first time hitting a golf ball and, contrary to his usual competitive spirit, he kept a sense of proportion and fun despite being outperformed by Max's 6-year-old grandson. Yurii got to know lots of people through helping Max and Di's fundraising efforts for the Brain Tumour Charity in memory of their son Simon. On occasions Yurii would sit on their stall at the village fete and chat to anyone who showed interest, being particularly patient and helpful with younger children and older people. He also joined in the memorial walk with

Simon's friends and family to mark what would have been his 50th birthday.

If you can imagine an indulgent grandparent spoiling their grandchild before handing them back to their parents, that's how it was when Yurii stayed with Sally-Ann. She made no secret of the fact that he was her substitute son whilst her own son, Charlie, was living in the Far East. She also insisted that she would be stricter with him if he was living with her permanently, but that was a hypothetical statement. So when I heard that she'd told him not to catch the 303 into Worcester as she would give him a lift in and that she'd sometimes give him spending money, I just had to shake my head like a despairing parent who knows that the grandparent is spoiling the child and that the battle has already been lost. It wasn't an actual issue, just an opportunity to make fun of our different parenting styles with Yurii.

Yurii was the beneficiary of both Sally-Ann's empty nest instincts and her son Charlie's unwanted clothes. Plus on several occasions, if Sally-Ann was away, Yurii was invited to join her husband David for a pub meal. They both enjoyed those outings and I would later hear a detailed description from Yurii about the marvels of what they'd each had to eat. But the most useful role that David played, from my point of view, was giving Yurii an early morning lift to Birmingham airport on the couple of occasions when he went to Poland to meet his family or to the Ukrainian Embassy in Warsaw to sort out passport issues. David was an early riser and petrol-head so giving him a passenger and a reason for hitting the road was almost doing him a favour. Well it was certainly doing me a favour.

Sally and Steve were the third couple who hosted Yurii when we were away. I had known Sally in her professional capacity as a physiotherapist back in the 1990s but, shortly after this, she moved away from the village for about twenty years. The next time I saw her was at the first SUN meeting in 2022, by which point she was retired and had moved back to Ombersley. To be sure that Yurii didn't get confused between Sally and Sally-Ann (and a third Sally who worked at Kingsway), I started to refer to Sally as Tall Sally and that soon became Long Tall Sally. She and Steve lived in the centre of the village, only a few doors down from the old bakery. Outside their neat, new redbrick house was a lovely display of potted hydrangeas in pinks and blues and mauves. Yurii was often left in charge of watering the flowers and tomatoes when Sally and Steve were away and he took his job seriously – typically taking hours over each visit. He set himself high standards and whether he was playing tennis, making soup or looking after someone's garden, he expected to do a first-class job.

Once Yurii turned 18 and was officially signed off by Children's Services, I gave him a choice for when we went away: he could move in with one of the SUN team as previously or he could stay at our house on his own and just go out for dinner. He chose the latter which gave me the opportunity, as his PA, to create yet another rota. He'd arrive home from school to an empty house, get changed, check the dinner rota to see where he was eating then off he'd go to have a sociable meal with one of the team. It worked out very well for everyone.

The activities of SUN supported the families and individuals who had arrived to the safety of our village and, generally, the horrors of war were far removed from all our daily lives. But occasionally there was a connection to the ongoing death and destruction that left us stunned. When Ania, the entrepreneurial English teacher detailed earlier, heard the devastating news that her friend Kostya had been killed in action, Sally was with her. The shock of Ania's grief was compounded by knowing that Kostya had left a widow, Tania aged only 32, and two young daughters. The tragic waste of life that was taking place on an epic scale was now embodied in the death of this one young man.

Sally wanted to do something to help Kostya's broken family so she invited them to come to the UK on holiday and they accepted. She helped with their visas, met them from the airport and decorated her home with Ukrainian flags to welcome them. After a couple of days in Ombersley she took them to Mousehole in Cornwall for a week where she had rented a holiday home on the harbour for the family and Ania whilst she and Steve stayed in a little cottage nearby. The little girls explored the rock pools and played on the beach; they all hiked up St Michael's Mount; they enjoyed Cornish pasties, fish and chips and ice-cream. They stayed in the UK for a further 4 weeks whilst Sally organised a schedule of activities to keep everyone entertained. At the end of their stay, full of lovely memories and gratitude, they returned to Ukraine and the bleak reality of the ongoing attacks from Russia and life without Kostya.

Chapter 23
Summer Jobs

'He's a really smart lad,' I said to Paul, one of the tenants at Kingsway House, as we chatted by the coffee machine. 'His English is amazing and he's doing maths and computer science at A level.' Paul nodded, sipped his latte, asked a few more questions about Yurii then suggested he send in his CV. The tech company he worked for, Sentinel, was always interested in bright young things who were IT savvy, even those who just wanted a summer job.

The school summer holidays were fast approaching and I wanted Yurii to have something constructive to do. He'd tried to pick up work in his first summer with us, but what he found was little more than a few gardening jobs amounting to four or five hours per week. This meant he had no reason to get out of bed before the afternoon, so he'd be having breakfast not long before I'd be cooking dinner. The sun would be shining outside, but he'd be inside plugged in to his Play Station and it seemed that every time I walked past the TV there was a cartoon horse galloping across the screen going nowhere fast. That horse summed up my feeling of frustration with the situation, but I tried to keep such negativity to myself as Yurii didn't have the usual range of options that British teenagers had.

In Kyiv his school summer holidays would have played out very differently. With all his schoolfriends, basketball mates and relatives living in the city, he would have had lots of options. Not only that, but his home was in a capital city with so much to do within cycling or walking distance and good public transport for other things. In contrast, Ombersley had an hourly bus service into Worcester or Kidderminster and the last bus got back to the village at 7 pm. There was no bus to Droitwich and the road was totally unsuitable for cycling so, if he wanted to go there, he had to rely on a lift or do a tortuous, 2-sides-of-a-triangle journey and catch a bus to Worcester and then a train back to Droitwich.

I don't think that socialising with his age group was top of his agenda but, had he wanted to, his choices were limited as his close friends were in Austria and Cambridge. According to his form tutor he was well liked at school, but this hadn't resulted in any friendships that I was aware of and no invitations to parties or other teenage gatherings. Similarly he played tennis and basketball with young people but this didn't lead to anything outside practices and matches. In fact he seemed most comfortable mixing with Rick's and my friends and most of us were old enough to be his grandparents. On top of that he was staunchly against alcohol so his life outside school was a world away from that of typical British teenagers.

You would think that he would have jumped at the chance to meet Ukrainians of a similar age to him. You would be wrong. There was a Ukrainian family living near us which included a 16-year-old boy. By the time they moved in, Yurii was settled in to school, knew plenty of people in Ombersley, knew his way around Worcester and was a fluent and confident speaker of English. Yet he was very resistant to visiting them and seeing if he could help in any way. I had to be very firm and remind him of all the help he had received and now it was his turn to do what he could to help others – to pay it forward.

It was the same story with a young Ukrainian teenager, Nikita, whom I'd placed with a family in Worcester. I asked Yurii to meet up with him and show him around, 'I don't think he needs my help. He'll be fine,' he replied, knowing nothing about this boy. Again it took a firm reminder that life is about giving and not just taking before he agreed to meet up with the newly arrived teenager. In each case the help he gave was a one-off and nothing more came of it. He seemed to close the door on a possible friendship before even meeting these boys and it baffled me. For a while I wondered if it was because they were Ukrainian and he didn't want to be reminded of home. But in due course he did make friends with two Ukrainians that I got to know, Artem and Veronika. They both came with their families under the Homes for Ukraine scheme; Veronika eventually became his girlfriend which transformed his social life. Both Artem and Veronika lived in rural villages, each in opposite directions from Ombersley, that were so poorly served by public transport that walking the ten miles to meet up with them would have been quicker than trying to get there by bus. I felt for these teenagers who were all dependent on adults giving them lifts; back in Kyiv they would have been independent. It didn't even register on the scale of Putin's crimes, but he had stolen a chunk of what should have been their carefree years.

As Yurii's second summer approached, for his sake as well as mine, I wanted him to have some structure to his days. I wanted him to have a reason for getting out of bed but I also wanted him to learn some new skills, gain experience to add to his university application and earn some money. When I first mentioned the possibility of a summer job with Sentinel, his response was pure Yurii:

'I don't think I'll apply yet. I don't think they'll find anyone else.'

He didn't know what the job was, he didn't know anyone from Sentinel and he didn't even know if they were advertising for anyone. Sometimes I just had to breathe, breathe, breathe to cope with Yurii.

Anyway, at some point he decided he would like to apply for a job with Sentinel so he needed to create a CV. We had a laugh trying to turn nothing into something:

Experience in reptile care: Skilled in daily care & welfare of exotic species. Demonstrated reliability and common sense.

Experience in gardening: Skilled in identifying and removing weeds; skilled in estimating correct level of hydration for potted plants. Showed reliability and commitment to mundane tasks.

Experience in moving furniture: Skilled in relocation of office furniture including up and down stairs and through narrow spaces. Showed physical stamina and ability to take instructions and work as a member of a team.

Experience in bar work: Skilled in serving a wide variety of alcoholic and non-alcoholic drinks. Skilled in choosing correct glass. Able to take part in friendly small talk whilst working.

I don't know if Sentinel were more persuaded by his reliability in looking after tortoises or by his ability with maths and computers, but they invited him for an interview. This went well and he landed himself a summer job, testing code, which started the day before he turned 18. The casual, branded preppy outfits that came his way via Charlie, Sally-Ann's son, suited him and helped him look the part for his office-based job.

On Yurii's 18th birthday Rick and I took him to The Cross Keys in the village for dinner, along with some neighbours and their son. Despite everyone urging him to mark his entry into adulthood with a drink, alcohol was an absolute red line for him. A few days later we invited Team Yurii from SUN to join us for tea and cakes to celebrate his 18th and to thank them for their help. These people had given him lifts to and from basketball and/or had given him bed and board at times when Rick and I were away on holiday. They made life easier for Yurii and for me so it was an opportunity to get to know them a bit better. Although we'd done our best to make his 18th birthday as special as it could be in the circumstances, he should have been with his family and friends in his own country.

Chapter 24
Sixth Form Graduation

The parents of RGS upper sixth formers were gathering outside Perrins Hall in the warm evening sunshine. They stood in small groups chatting whilst waiting for the signal to enter the hall for the graduation ceremony. I stood slightly apart as an observer whilst memories flashed through my mind; it had been 12 years since I had attended such an event for my youngest child and 27 years since my oldest child had started at the school. During those times I had known a good few of the parents and staff, but today I only recognised the headmaster - and he was the third RGS headmaster I had known. I felt separate and different. Back then I was a parent but now I was …. well I wasn't sure what to call myself. Technically I was Yurii's sponsor but that sounded very cold.

We'd had a minor spat the day before when he'd told me he planned to go to the cinema with his girlfriend on this particular evening. I reminded him that it was the final occasion of his RGS life; I had accepted the school's invitation for both of us and not attending would be disrespectful. To be fair I don't think he really appreciated that it was such a significant occasion. I think he considered it an optional extra like the school prom which he had opted out of. Things became a bit heated but he got the message and rearranged his social calendar. As it turned out, it was a very good thing that he did.

I took my seat in the wood panelled hall whilst Yurii joined the other pupils to sit in the gallery behind me. A sixth former played some gentle piano pieces as the hall gradually filled with parents and other guests. Teachers in black academic gowns gathered on the stage or moved purposefully around the hall trailing authority in their wake.

Flicking through the programme, I noted all the different cups and awards and prizes; for music, acting, debating, sports, contributions to school life and the full range of academic subjects. It all looked very impressive. I picked Yurii out of the year group photo then skimmed through the programme once more. That was when I saw his name next to an award: The Wareing Cup for Overcoming Adversity. Wow – I wasn't expecting that and obviously he wasn't either or he wouldn't have planned to go to the cinema.

As the school clock finished chiming 7pm, the Chair of Governors started his welcome address. Some of the guests on the stage behind him tried to cool down by using the programme as a fan. Meanwhile the pupils were being lined up offstage so that they all appeared at the right time for the right award. The clapping and cheering came in waves with a slight tailing off of applause as one group of prize winners left the stage then surged again as the next group replaced them. As Yurii came up for his prize I didn't know whether to film him or clap so made a bit of a mess of both.

Once all the awards had been given out, the Guest of Honour, an ex-pupil, made an entertaining speech, no doubt exaggerating his unruly behaviour back in the day. The occasion concluded with the Headmaster's summary of the year. It was all very traditional, very precise and very British.

And then I was outside again sitting on a bench in the sunshine waiting for Yurii to appear. As the clock chimed 8 pm, I was approached by a member of staff who seemed to know who I was and introduced herself as one of the maths teachers. She hadn't actually taught Yurii but she knew him well and was full of admiration for him. Whilst she was singing his praises, his form teacher came over to introduce herself and she too wanted to tell me that Yurii was very well liked in his tutor group and that she thought very highly of him herself. Not for the first time, I felt a sense of maternal pride in him even though I wasn't his mother and couldn't take any credit for his behaviour.

Then Yurii himself appeared with a very sizeable and impressive looking trophy which he was to share with Ira, the other Ukrainian in the upper sixth. So of course there were photos taken with her, with me, with members of staff and on his own. Behind us, in the central quad, elegant tables were laid with exquisite looking refreshments; parents, pupils and staff were milling around eating and chatting. I asked Yurii if he would like to get something to eat or drink but he declined. I think he felt the same as me; we were both a bit different and didn't quite fit in to this particular situation – each for different reasons. It was time to go.

On the way home I reflected on the immense journey Yurii had been on since leaving Kyiv in February 2022. Not just physically but emotionally, culturally and academically. He'd left as a 16-year-old whilst Putin's tanks were poised to attack his home city. He'd left behind everyone and everything he knew and loved and had headed off on his own into the unknown. He'd crossed Europe relying on the kindness of strangers to help him on his way. Fate had meant that he'd ended up living with Rick and me.

He'd fitted into our family and our lifestyle and was friendly with lots of people in our village. He'd joined the sixth form of a very academic school, successfully adapted to a very different type of education, completed A level courses in three subjects in his second language and had offers to study computer science at two top British universities. It was all very impressive and he deserved his prize for overcoming adversity. Putin had upended his life but he hadn't ruined it.

Now 19 years old, his third summer in the UK was just beginning. He wanted a more relaxed summer than the previous one where he'd worked full time for Sentinel. He wanted to spend more time with his girlfriend before going away to university. The village pubs didn't realise what an asset he could have been behind the bar or waiting tables and didn't respond to his CV requesting work. But whilst waiting for his exam results, he managed to pick up a few odd jobs here and there.

The BBC news led on August 15th 2024 with A level results so, before I'd even got out of bed, my phone was pinging with texts from friends and family asking how Yurii had got on. The answer was staring me in the face as soon as I went downstairs to the kitchen – his eyes were shining with excitement and he had a great big smile on his face. He'd done it! He'd soon be off to the University of Sussex to begin the next phase of his life.

Although Yurii's departure would mean the official end of our relationship under the Homes for Ukraine scheme, it wouldn't mean the end of our relationship. For a start there were the university holidays when he'd need a home to return to; he had become one of our family and we would always be his anchor in Britain. But one day his country would be free of the Russian invaders and he'd be needed back home to help rebuild Ukraine and reconnect with his family and friends.

Considering he'd found himself in circumstances that he hadn't sought, he'd made the most of the opportunities on offer and had grown in so many ways since he'd left his family and set off into the unknown. He was well aware of the large number of people who had helped him on his journey from Kyiv to the point he was at now. In his personal statement for his university application, he used the phrase 'pay it forward', explaining that was what he wanted to do. At some point he would be in a position to give help to others and I hoped that's what he'd do. That's what we all have to do.

Chapter 25
Feedback from Hosts

'If you'd like to come to the UK, I'd be happy to sponsor you,' I had said in February 2022 as I stood by my office window on Foregate Street, trying to get the best phone signal. The words had come out of my mouth before I'd had time to discuss this particular situation with Rick. The 16-year-old on the end of the phone, Yurii, was in Switzerland at the time and through a chain of connections we were talking to each other. Cold shivers ran down my arms as I was talking to this young boy who had left Kyiv when the bombing started and was now travelling alone through Europe looking for somewhere safe to live. Telling him that he could have a home with us was the natural thing to do. I didn't need to think about it.

At that point I knew his name, age and nationality and he obviously spoke good English. Apart from that, he was a complete stranger. Luckily for us it turned out that hosting this particular unaccompanied teenager was as easy as hosting could ever be. Yurii was very independent, sociable, polite and considerate. He was also very bright and had a good sense of humour. He gave us our personal space as he wanted his own personal space. He adapted to our way of life very quickly and absorbed cultural differences at speed. There was no conflict over the use of the kitchen as I always did the cooking. There was no conflict over fridge space as I always did the shopping. Rick and I were the clear and only sources of authority in the home so there was no conflict between us and a parent.

Hosting Yurii was pretty lightweight compared to what some host families had taken on. Linda from Wellesbourne in Warwickshire took in a mother (Andriy's wife) and her newborn twins and later the grandmother too. Karen, also from Wellesbourne, gave a home to a mother and daughter plus her friend and their two cats. Sue from Dorset took in a pregnant woman. There really were some staggeringly generous people who put their homes and privacy on the line in order to help.

In the first few months of the war I found homes for 44 adults, 34 children, 2 dogs and 2 cats. However, by the summer of 2022 the first rush of enthusiasm for hosting under the Homes for Ukraine scheme dried up to almost nothing. It was disappointing to tell people that I was unlikely to be able to find them a sponsor although I would try. I felt particularly upset that I couldn't help Liudmila who had acted as an intermediary for me in Ukraine and helped with translating whenever necessary. By the time she was ready to leave with her two grandchildren, I couldn't find anywhere for her to stay.

For the vast majority who stayed in contact with me, hosting was a very positive experience and the following comments are just a selection:

Ginny, Wellesbourne, Warwickshire
Hosted Yuliia for 9 months

I was very fortunate indeed to welcome a delightful 52 year old Ukrainian lady into our house. She was the most considerate guest, thoroughly polite and charming. I was very, very fortunate to have such a lovely person stay with us.

Brian & Deirdre, Worcester
Hosta Olga for 2.5 years

We have found the experience to be very life enhancing and feel privileged that we were in a position to help. It has been an amazing journey watching and nurturing Olga's development in the UK as she is always studying, learning and working at something, forever growing in confidence and adapting to a brand new life here without her Ukrainian family. She is a qualified and experienced radiologist but works as a GP's assistant. We'll miss her when she leaves to go to university.

Fiona, Flyford Flavell, Worcestershire
Hosted Olena and 2 sons, Ruslan and Makar, for 9 months

Our experience was entirely positive. We were extremely lucky: Olena is a wonderful person and the children friendly and good fun.

Caroline, Totnes, Devon
Hosted Anna for 2 years and ongoing

Our Ukrainian visitor is still with us. She is very independent, already spoke English when she arrived, and quite quickly got a job in a local restaurant. Her routine is very different to ours (we have a 2 year old and a newborn) so we don't share mealtimes or hang out regularly, but it's lovely having her here. It's quite like a house share - nice chats when everyone is around but our own separate lives as well.

Julie and Andrew, Leamington Spa, Warwick
Hosted Yurii and Olena for 6 months

Our guests, Yurii and Olena arrived in June 2022. They were the same age as us, 61 and 56 - and that might have had something to do with how easy it was to welcome them into our home. That and the fact that we had children of similar ages, shared political interests and our values were pretty much aligned. Yurii's English was conversationally good and Olena, like us, relied on the Say Hi App to communicate. They both worked on improving their language skills during their 6 month stay; they became part of the local church community and quickly assimilated into village life. Olena took a job at the local pub and Yurii helped out neighbours and continued his political work in Ukraine, from afar.

Our experience of hosting was entirely positive. As the war progressed, and the news from home became more difficult to digest, hours spent around the kitchen table were about holding both the darker and the lighter sides of life in plain sight. We listened as they recounted the horror of Olena's father's home in Kherson being shelled; we raised shots of tequila and said plenty of 'Budmars' to the end of the conflict; we laughed over steaming bowlfuls of Olena's borscht. Somehow, acknowledging both the agony and the pleasures of life, was the pattern that defined our time together.

We said farewell to them in December of the same year and when some people asked us, 'Wasn't it difficult, sharing your home for that long?', our answer was always a definitive ''No'. Yurii and Olena were our gifts. Their kindness, generosity and humour were a daily reminder of what matters most in life. When they left, we gave them a souvenir key-ring and a key to our front door for them to keep. It was a small gesture, but one that we hoped would remind them of the friendship we share - and that our home is always theirs, too.'

Fran, Flushing, Cornwall
Hosted Lina for 18 months

She is an absolute star, I'm SO proud of her as she is now at Salford University about to start a degree in graphic design. She is really looking forward to her course. I can't wait to visit when she is settled.

Linda, Wellesbourne, Warwickshire
Hosted Alla and her baby twin boys for 1 year and 10 months

They arrived May 2022 when the boys were barely 12 weeks old. It was a success from the start and Alla quickly became like one of the family even calling me her English mum! In May 2023 they were joined by Lessia, Alla's mum, who came primarily to help Alla with the then 15 month old boys. Lessia not surprisingly at 63 found it harder to settle and had very little English. We meet most weeks & I still support them when needed mainly with paperwork. We have a lovely relationship. I am really glad I took them in, they are more like extended family now!

Jim & Janis, Pershore, Worcestershire
Hosted Olena, her son and her mother for 13 months

We have enjoyed the experience and have never fallen out with any of them in all that time. We would do it again if needed.

Chris & Kathy, Wotton-under-Edge, Gloucestershire
Hosted Oksana and Tamila for 6 months

We are pleased to let you know that we had a wonderful experience hosting Oksana and Tamila who stayed with us for about 5-6 months in 2022.

After they left us and moved back to Ukraine, Tamila returned to the UK and moved into the university halls to start a foundation year at Bristol University to study Law, which she successfully completed earlier this year. Tamila will be returning in the next few weeks to start her 4-year degree course at Bristol. We regularly meet up with Tamila in Bristol, and occasionally with Oksana when she is visiting, and Kathy sometimes meets with Tamila to go to an exhibition or a writer's talk.

Fiona and Mike, Molesworth, Cambridgeshire
Hosted Iulia, Oleksandr and son aged 8 for 17 months

Overall we thought it was a life affirming experience, one we went into as most people probably did with some anxieties. We found it interesting, educational, uplifting and positive. They were always so grateful for everything and never took us for granted or complained.

Eileen and Mike, Ombersley, Worcestershire
Hosted Ania for 1 year

She very quickly became part of the family and slotted seamlessly into our household ..... she was immensely popular in the village as a translator for other families whose Ukrainian guests spoke little English. However, her popularity wasn't solely due to her linguistic skills: Ania has a very warm, bubbly personality which is very endearing.

Name and location withheld , Worcestershire
Hosted for 2 years

I felt responsible for her social life as she is utterly alone here. I also felt a responsibility for safeguarding when she made some personally naive decisions. I feel I do not have the capacity to do this again it has been a pretty intensive 2 years.

Name and location withheld, Worcestershire
Hosted a family of 5 for 2.5 years and ongoing

They are a very pleasant and amenable group of people. The parents work hard doing a variety of casual jobs and the children go to school. None of them have made great progress with their English but we manage with Google translate. The mother sometimes cooks for us and they are all generally helpful and nice to have around.

D and M, Worcestershire
Hosted Natalie and daughter Sonia for 4 months

It was a success in that we were able to provide a refuge for Natalie and Sonia while they were here. The best bits were that both of them were friendly and tried their best to fit in. However they seemed to spend most of the time in the house in their bedrooms communicating with friends on their phones. We felt a bit disappointed that they rarely joined us other than to take family meals.

Fiona and Andrew, Nr Tenbury Wells, Worcestershire
Hosted Alla for 1 year and ongoing

She has now been with us for a year and we can't believe how lucky we have been! She has slotted into the family and it feels like she has been here longer. My daughter calls her my fourth child! We are moving and she is happy to come with us.

Kate and Keith, Weston-super-Mare, Somerset
Hosted Luda, Yana and Ivan for 3 months then hosted Viktor and Olesia for 22 months and ongoing

We were sceptical about having a second refugee family but how glad I am that we agreed! Viktor and Olesia are the most delightful couple, I love them to bits! Viktor constantly makes me laugh even though his English is limited. You ask what the worst bits are …… when they go on holiday, we miss them! The best bits … they are sharing our home which is now their home. What a wonderful couple they are, thank you for connecting them with us.

Karen, Wellesbourne, Warwickshire
Hosted Alina, her daughter Iryna and their 2 cats. Also Iryna's friend Katya for 4 months.

From the get-go it worked. I had a two-storey holiday let (our former garage) which was perfect for all the girls for their privacy and to be able to relax from the turmoil they'd temporarily left behind. I was incredibly impressed by all the girls' application and ability to continue their working lives thanks to the internet. Their stoicism and dedication to what they do despite the horrendous events in their own country is exemplary. Overall they have been a lesson to us all in my family. We've had laughter and tears and have spent, and are still spending, many happy hours together. Their kindness and generosity is unparalleled. We'll never lose touch with each other and have vowed once the war is over I'll be travelling to see them in their home. I can't wait - in more ways than one.

When Karen sent me her feedback (above), she also forwarded this message to her from Alina:

I have been missing you a lot. I still can't believe how lucky I am to have met you in that tough period in my life. You know I am always active and trying to push away my memories about that horrible time. But as soon as I recollect in my mind the first days in England I start crying and feeling so grateful to you and all the people who supported me and my girls at that time. I always felt support from the people around me. It was so important for all of us.

Giving a home to desperate strangers fleeing war is a risk – you have no idea how it's going to work out until you give it a go. But wouldn't we all rather be in the position of offering a home than seeking one?

Letter from Yurii published in the October 2024 edition of the *Ombersley and Doverdale Parish Magazine*

Living in Ombersley   September 8th 2024

My name is Yurii, and I am a Ukrainian refugee who came to Britain after the Russian invasion. I've lived in Ombersley for the past two and a half years, attended RGS, passed my A-Levels, and now I'm going to the University of Sussex in Brighton to study computer science.

Before I leave, I thought it would be a great idea to write a thank you article in the parish magazine about how grateful I am for the luck and opportunity to be living in a lovely place like Ombersley. After the invasion of Ukraine I have lived with Sue and Rick Johns and got the chance to know many more wonderful people in the village.

From the start I was invited to various events and festivities which made me realise how strong and connected the local community is. Everyone seems to get involved and support each other. I felt included and respected by people of all ages. Ombersley & Doverdale Tennis Club gave me the chance to learn how to play tennis and attend regular practices. I had a really good time and made some of my first friends and connections there which I really valued .

Local people gave me the opportunity to earn some pocket money by helping with various small jobs like watering plants or lawn mowing, even looking after tortoises. At all times, there were people checking up on me curious to know about how my family is doing and my personal well-being. Countless times I was offered support, financial or emotional, and on a few occasions people took me out for dinner, and I appreciated the opportunity to try tasty food from our local pubs.

There were things I couldn't have done on my own. For instance, with my passion for basketball, I wouldn't have been able to go to practices if I didn't have people who volunteered to give me a lift. What impressed me even more is that it would always be late evening hours, despite it being a normal time to have your dinner, they still showed up for me.

Whenever Sue and Rick were away, I was kindly invited to stay with other village friends who I ought to mention. Max and Diane Seivewright, Sally-Ann and David Beckett, Sally Robertson-Smith and Steve Johnson. Many thanks for allowing me to live with you as long as it was needed I really appreciated it.

I've never seen a community like this before and I'm always happy when somebody asks me, something like, where do you live in England because I get an opportunity to tell them all about a wonderful place called Ombersley. I have received so much help since leaving Kyiv in 2022 that I hope one day to be able to pay it forward and help others in need.

Chapter 26
Kyiv, Ukraine – July 2024

A line of children and medics stumbled away from the smouldering rubble behind them. Some of the children were dragging IV drips behind them, some of the medics were carrying the little ones who were too ill to walk. The bald-headed children, already battling disease, now had another battle on their hands: the inhumanity rained down on them by their Russian neighbours. Adults and children all had the blank look of the traumatised.

Those who had come to help looked on in disbelief at what was left of Ohmatdyt Children's Hospital in Kyiv. Hundreds of local people, incongruous in their shorts and flip-flops, worked alongside professional rescue services to form a human chain and pass bricks along the line, one at a time, to try and clear away some of the rubble. The horror of who might be trapped underneath went unspoken; it was too appalling to contemplate people entombed under tonnes of masonry. Every now and then a shout of 'Tysha!' went up – a call for silence to check for human sounds.

Doctors who had been in the middle of performing paediatric surgery were now looking on in a daze at what had been their workplace. This was where the savers of life met the bringers of death. Medics in scrubs or white coats sobbed as they spoke into their phones trying to articulate the atrocity in front of them. Words were hard to find. Silence and ragged breathing, punctuated by swearing, conveyed the abomination they were witnessing.

It was July 8th 2024 and these scenes propelled Ukraine back to the top of the news agenda. Until this horrifying attack, it seemed that the media had got bored by the apparent stalemate. Back in February 2022 we had all watched with astonishment as the 30-mile-long Russian convoy, poised to attack Kyiv, stalled. Unbelievably the invaders, so used to the harshest weather conditions in their own country, had come ill-prepared for a Ukrainian winter. Pictures showed tanks with the wrong tyres stuck in the mud. Stories emerged of the Russians lacking food, fuel, ammunition and maps. Instead of rolling in and capturing the capital city with ease, the terrifying column of tanks turned itself into a massive military traffic jam. Meanwhile the Ukrainians, brave, spirited and angry, showed that they had absolutely no intention of allowing the enemy to take any of their land without a fight. It was thrilling to watch the humiliating retreat of Putin's army from Kyiv and to consider that this war could be over quickly.

Unfortunately Putin's initial military miscalculation just meant that, in addition to his obsession with bringing Ukraine back into a new Russian Empire, he now also had to demonstrate that the retreat from Kyiv was strategic and that his armies were unbeatable. For the next few years the Russians pummelled Ukraine whilst President Zelensky did his best to keep the world's focus on the war. Dressed in military fatigues to remind everyone of his country's existential struggle, he spoke to parliaments around the world, his words powerful and moving. But the standing ovations that followed were not enough. European countries understood that Ukraine was on the front line fighting against Russian imperialism; if it fell then other countries would follow. We had seen the template with Hitler. But the Europeans had a queasiness around war and death which was no match for the Russian President's ease with mass slaughter; his war machine had vast manpower to use as cannon fodder. The Europeans and NATO sent warm words and arms to Ukraine and strongly worded warnings to Russia. Words of support were all very well but Zelensky wanted permission to use his allies' weapons to attack the enemy on its own territory. Despite the president's begging, permission was denied for fear that the war would escalate or that the short-tempered tyrant would push the nuclear button.

As the exhausted Ukrainians went on to the back foot, fighting a defensive war, the world's attention moved on to other things. From October 2023 the war in Gaza saw the media moving their resources to report on this new and horrifying conflict. The number of reports from Ukraine dwindled and it took exceptional atrocities for reporters to return. The July 2024 attack on the children's hospital had one positive outcome: it reminded the world that the Ukrainians were still fighting and that their enemy continued to commit monstrous war crimes.

Some of us had never forgotten the war in Ukraine as we were still hosting Ukrainians. By the time of the hospital attack, Yurii had been with us for nearly two and a half years – much longer than most people on the Homes for Ukraine scheme. The idea behind the scheme was for hosts to support refugees for 6 - 12 months whilst helping them to find jobs and independent accommodation. This was all very well for adults and families but Yurii, still a schoolboy, did not fit into those categories. The right thing for us to do was to keep him until he'd left school and either gone to university or got a job. We were happy to do this, but I was conscious that he was getting more and more distant from his own culture and values and his country's wartime struggles. Since leaving his home in February 2022, he had met up with his mother and other family members in Poland on two occasions, but his father was of fighting age and therefore not allowed to leave the country. The only contact he had with his son was by phone and video calls. Yurii was having a traditional British education, living our comfortable lifestyle, mixing with our friends and probably being influenced by our values. Although he had plenty of friends amongst our generation, he lacked the equivalence of his teenage friendship group from Kyiv. We could only guess at how different his life might have been if the war had never happened.

Yurii in particular, but thousands of people on Homes for Ukraine visas, received an incredible amount of support from British taxpayers and from other organisations and individuals. In fact by July 2024, 188,100 people had been granted visas under the scheme and absorbed into British families all over the UK. Hosting was a way of showing support for the country which was fighting for democracy for all of us. It was also a way of acknowledging that, but for Putin, these people would have been living their preferred lives in their own homes in their home country with their families and friends. They were in the UK for safety not as a lifestyle choice.

The Homes for Ukraine scheme was a generous idea that was initially hampered by government ministers who didn't really believe in it and local officials who didn't really understand it. But even though it was flawed, it highlighted two important points: there were thousands of people in the UK who were prepared to share their homes with refugees and that this was a far more humane way of helping scared and vulnerable people than putting them into cramped hotels and offshore barges.

If it worked for Ukrainians, it could work for refugees from other countries. Dispersing people into towns and villages throughout the country would get rid of the stigma of refugee hostels and hotels and avoid overburdening particular areas with large numbers of temporary residents awaiting Home Office decisions. Volunteer families on the Homes for Ukraine scheme were given 'thank you' payments of £350/month and asked to commit to 6 months hosting. This was enough money to cover the basic costs of the hosts but not enough to attract people to host for the wrong reasons. If the scheme was extended to other refugees, home checks could be carried out by local authorities as they were under Homes for Ukraine, but with a lighter touch. And temporary visas could be issued in the same way as they were for Ukrainians which could be extended or revoked accordingly.

And surely there must be a way of harnessing the amazing localised support for Ukrainian refugees, like our SUN group, to create a network of hubs throughout the country? Setting up a government department to oversee homes for refugees could be a starting point. Ombersley set up its own little network through which many people gave support in terms of services and goods. Because we only had a small number of refugees in our village, people like Yurii ended up with more than their fair share. If donors could register offers of help or goods to a hub serving a larger area then it could be distributed more evenly. Using the Homes for Ukraine scheme as a template, we could transform our approach to housing refugees and save British taxpayers a lot of money. It could be a solution to a political and moral problem.

Chapter 27
Ukraine – November 2024

Kherson is one of the unfortunate cities where a dystopian video game plays out regularly in real life. On the screen the crosshairs lock on to the pedestrian crossing the road. Silently the man falls to the ground and the crosshairs move on to a car which then careers off the road in a puff of smoke. A cyclist is progressing purposefully along a road next to a river until the drone pilot chooses to exterminate him. Lying on the ground, the cyclist's anguish goes unheard by his killer. In this sick war, Putin's army kills civilians to terrorise the population.

Meanwhile in central Kyiv, the weak winter sun in the pale blue sky is a diluted version of the national colours of Ukraine. A young woman stands in Maidan Square staring at a vast bright blue and yellow sea of fluttering, rippling flags. Behind her the two hundred foot tall Independence Monument is a reminder of why her country is under attack and why her husband is now dead. In her hand is the national flag with a photo of the man who was father to their two children. She had wanted to write something fitting on the card, to convey a sense of the man she had lost, but the task had defeated her and she had simply written, 'Jaroslav – we love you'. She thinks carefully before placing her tribute between two flags: one is a memorial to another soldier, so that her husband could be with a comrade. The other shows a photograph of a smiling little girl, the same age as their daughter. War kills indiscriminately. Leaving him here with strangers is hard. Going home without him is harder.

In nearby cafes and crowded shops, life appears to go on as normal. But there are signs of war everywhere: soldiers in uniform, posters recruiting drone pilots, windows taped to prevent them breaking, a destroyed tank. Every citizen is now an expert on the difference between drones and missiles, when to move and when to stay put. In school classrooms children expect to evacuate to a safe area up to three times per day. No one goes to bed or takes a bath without planning for a hasty exit should the siren sound. Everyone is on edge, nothing can be taken for granted.

For those who choose to stay in Ukraine or who can't leave, there is constant anxiety: fear for personal safety, fear for the safety of loved ones, fear of the news. For those who came to the UK, their personal safety is assured but their other fears are the same. Plus they have different problems to deal with: living with strangers, fitting in to a new culture, learning a new language, adapting to a new school system, finding work, finding friends, homesickness, the stigma of being described as a refugee when you're used to working for a living and having your own home. Even for those who had a positive experience with the Homes for Ukraine scheme, can you ever really feel any more than a visitor in another family's home? Can you ever behave exactly as you would in your own home?

One day millions of people who left Ukraine will return to an exhausted and broken country. Of those who stayed, some will have been killed. Many of those who survived will have lived through unimaginable horrors. Those who chose to fight or were obliged to fight will, rightfully, be considered heroes by those who couldn't or didn't. Everyone will have experienced loss: everyone will have lost family, friends, colleagues or neighbours; everyone will have lost homes, businesses or security; everyone will have lost the easy confidence that comes with living in a country at peace. Those who left and those who stayed will have to learn to live with each other again.

As the war slogs on towards its third anniversary, Putin's tactic of attrition appears to be paying off. He has no shortage of Russians to send to the so-called meat-grinder of the battlefield and he even has access now to fresh North Korean troops. He has recently hosted a conference in Moscow of 9 countries belonging to the BRICS group (including China, India and South Africa) proving that he is not the globally isolated, pariah figure that the West would like him to be. Donald Trump is returning to the White House and determined to end the war, probably by appeasing Putin. Ukraine and its allies are tired and disheartened.

If Putin gains some territory, it has come at a huge price to Russia: at least 70,000 troops have died and continue to die in action. Mainly young men with their lives ahead of them. Did they even know what they were fighting for? Do most Russians really believe that Zelensky, the country's first ever Jewish president, allowed Nazism to thrive in Ukraine and threaten their security?

Whatever the final outcome of the war, Ukrainians can be proud of standing up to their massive, autocratic neighbour in a David and Goliath fight. They are clear that they are fighting for their existence and the right to align with Europe should they so choose. Britain too can be proud that it provided military aid, political support and the Homes for Ukraine scheme. Offering refugees a home via the scheme gave some of us the framework to do something practical. Other people found other ways to help those whose lives had been devastated. As Albert Einstein said, 'The world is a dangerous place, not because of those who do evil, but because of those who look on and do nothing'.

Acknowledgements

I'd like to thank the following friends and family who read the early drafts of this book and gave me useful feedback and encouragement: Anna Johns, Toni Johns, Jan Stafford, Liz Brandon, Julie Langridge, Miranda Robbins, Ania Hlazkova, Anne Heron, Jo Richards, and Dave Roach.

I had Zoom calls with Matthieu Wagnières who looked after Yurii in Switzerland and Carla Chazottes who looked after him in Paris. Using their accounts of hosting Yurii combined with his own account, I created my version. Their generosity was crucial to Yurii's story turning out well.

I also had several video calls with Yurii's father, Sasha, who helped me understand some of the decisions Yurii made.

David Meddows provided the link to Olena P. who knew Yurii's father. In addition to being a lynchpin in this story, David also sent me some Whatsapps and other messages which helped me piece the timeline together.

I'd also like to thank Sian Smith of Sian Smith Editorial for her professional appraisal of my manuscript and subsequent copyediting She helped me understand how little I knew about the editorial process and was a valuable source of advice as well as being an independent sounding board.

Harvey Fitzhugh of Sleep. Create. Repeat. https://www.sleepcreaterepeat.co.uk/ designed the book cover without ever having met Yurii. All he knew was that he was a teenage Ukrainian boy yet he came up with an image that was breathtakingly like Yurii. When I showed Yurii the cover he replied, 'Wow – that looks like me! I've got a jacket like that! That's a Ukrainian train!' then he put on his jacket and did the pose to imitate the cover. Hats off to Harvey for getting such approval.

Thank you to Harvey Fitzhugh for creating the journey map, and to Harvey, Matthieu Wagnières, Carla Chazottes, Toni Johns and our local villagers in Ombersley for supplying pictures.

I'm grateful to Rick for taking on the technical side of publishing my account. He read a book on self-publishing, 'Self-Publish Your Book Like A Pro' by Becky Warrack and then did everything necessary to turn my manuscript into a book.

And finally, thank you to Yurii for allowing me to tell his story.

Yurii's Journey in Pictures

Helping out in Switzerland on a mini-digger (above), and in Paris with Serge (below)

Fresh off the Eurostar at St Pancras Station, London (above), and by the River Severn in Worcester on his first weekend (below)

First visit to the Royal Grammar School (RGS) Worcester (above), and learning how to iron his own clothes (below)

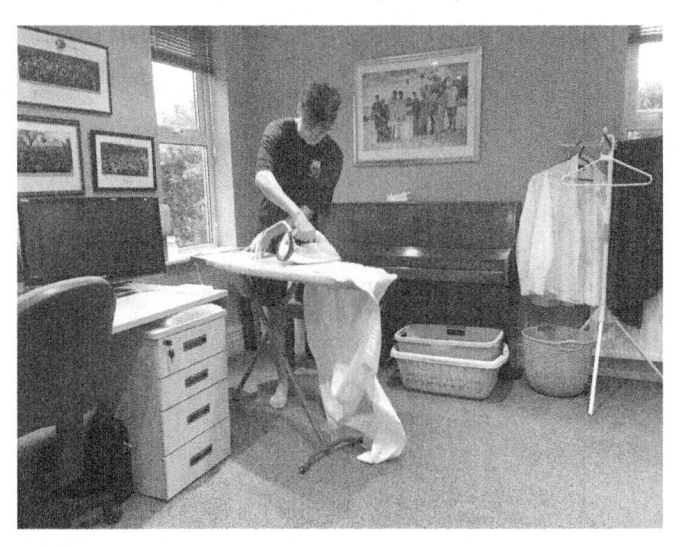

Ready to join the Sixth Form at RGS (above), and on the Malvern Hills with Barney and Bella (below)

Helping Max at the village fete (above), and having a golf lesson with Max and grandson (below)

Helping out on the bar at a Kingsway House charity event

Eighteenth birthday dinner with the neighbours at the Cross Keys pub, Ombersley (above), and recreating the book's cover pose (below)

With the author at the RGS Sixth Form
graduation (above), and all ready to leave
for university (below)

Printed in Great Britain
by Amazon